Gender Vertigo

Debbie Henderson

Barbara J. Risman

Gender Vertigo

american families in transition

Yale University Press   New Haven and London

Library of Congress Cataloging-in-Publication Data
Risman, Barbara J., 1956–
Gender vertigo : American families in transition /
Barbara J. Risman.
p. cm.
Includes bibliographical references and index.
ISBN 0-300-07215-5 (cloth : alk.paper)
ISBN 0-300-08083-2 (pbk.: alk.paper)
1. Family—United States.   2. Man-woman
relationships—United States.   3. Husband and wife—
United States.   4. Parent and child—United States.
5. Sex role—United States.   I. Title.
HQ535.R57   1998
306.85'0973—dc21   97-28857
CIP

Designed by Sonia Scanlon.
Set in Bulmer with Futura display
type by Tseng Information Systems, Inc.
Durham, North Carolina.
Printed in the United States of America by
Vail-Ballou Press, Binghamton, New York.

A catalogue record for this book is available from
the British Library.

The paper in this book meets the guidelines for
permanence and durability of the Committee on
Production Guidelines for Book Longevity of the
Council on Library Resources.

10 9 8 7 6 5 4 3 2

*In memory of and in dedication to my mother,
Gertrude Horvitz Risman*

A just future would be one without gender and its social structure and practices; one's sex would have no more relevance than one's eye color or the length of one's toes.
—Susan Moller Okin, *Justice, Gender and the Family*

We live in a world shaped by the collective failure of our forebears to abolish gender inequities. The corollary is that our children may also live in such a world.
—Robert W. Connell, *Gender and Power*

The prime paradox of gender is that in order to dismantle the institution you must first make it very visible.
—Judith Lorber, *Paradoxes of Gender*

Contents

Acknowledgments

The very possibility of a sociology for women can be credited to a previous generation of feminist scholars, who have created an academic climate in which feminist scholarship can exist and even thrive. If my work is critical of some of theirs, it nonetheless rests on the tremendous successes of the first generation of feminist scholars to legitimize gender as an academic specialty. To those scholars, I owe a debt of gratitude. Without them, the choices I have made would never have existed, even in my imagination.

There are many other people without whom this book would never have been written. I have had the remarkable good fortune of being born in the right place at the right time and of finding intellectual camaraderie throughout my career. My initial decision to reject the accepted androgyny theory of gender and to create my own theory was supported from my earliest days in graduate school by my mentors at the University of Washington, Pepper Schwartz and Philip Blumstein.

North Carolina State University has consistently provided me with the time and money to explore new ideas and begin new projects; the research reported in Chapters 3 and 4 was initially supported by college and university grants (and later by the National Science Foundation). I have also been blessed with departmental colleagues, particularly Maxine Atkinson and Donald Tomaskovic-Devey, with whom I share intellectual concerns, political passions, and deep friendships. Stephen Blackwelder, Kristen Myers, and Danette Johnson-Sumerford have provided excellent research assistance at different times during the data analysis, and all have become real partners through the years. Katherine Hyde has provided research assistance at the last minute, and always with excellence and speed.

Colleagues far from my Raleigh home have also been indispensable to my work. The feminist sisterhood I have found through my involvement with Sociologists for Women in Society has given me the courage to follow my heart and write new ideas boldly. I am grateful to belong to an intellectual community that provides such sustenance. I also owe a debt of gratitude to Judith Howard, Mary Romero, and Joey Sprague. We are editing a book series, and their constant friendship and companionship has made the task great fun. Our collaboration has made me a crisper writer and thinker. Their willingness to let me concentrate on this book when they might have preferred that my attention be turned to the *Gender Lens* series has been greatly appreciated. My relationship with Joey Sprague is proof that friendship can deepen in cyberspace. Without her, my e-mail messages might have been primarily distractions.

More colleagues than I can possibly thank have read drafts of chapters or commented on papers that eventually became part of this book. The following friends and colleagues read chapters more than once or read more than one chapter, providing invaluable help: Maxine Atkinson, Stephen Blackwelder, Judith Howard, Danette Johnson-Sumerford, Kristen Myers, Michael Schwalbe, and Donald Tomaskovic-Devey. Graduate students in my gender course at North Carolina State University have read drafts of this work over the years, and their reactions have helped shape it. Robert W. Connell and Joey Sprague read the entire manuscript, and it is much improved for their comments. I am indebted to them both. I have never met Sandra Bem, but reading her book *The Lenses of Gender* as I wrote this one gave me the courage to write in the first person. I also want to acknowledge my editor at Yale University Press, Gladys Topkis, who not only helped to sharpen my prose but who was understanding as the rest of my personal and professional responsibilities interfered with deadlines for this book. I also owe much thanks to Ahmed Aziz for his world-class secretarial support.

Finally, I want to thank Robert Connell for coining the phrase "gender vertigo" in the final chapter of his book *Masculinities* (1996) and for being so gracious when I requested his permission to use it in the title of this book. I have benefited much from the help of all these colleagues, taken much of their advice, and sometimes rejected it. The strengths of this book are clearly based on collective work; the weaknesses, alas, remain mine alone.

This book—indeed, my entire personal and professional life—is possible only because of the warmth and nurturance that I have always received in my most intimate relationships. I have lived a very privileged life, always having enough of what I need materially, as well as a great wealth of love. Parts of this book were written in my mother's home while I was caring for her during her final battle with cancer. I feel lucky to have work that I could fit around what was most important to me: sharing my mother's life with her, right to the end. The most important lesson I have learned, and from my mother, is that our post-gender families must elevate the traditionally female values of nurturing and homemaking above all else—for it is this work, what women have always done, that turns isolated individuals into families and communities, brick and mortar in hearth and home, and gives meaning to our lives. I want to acknowledge my mother's role in my intellectual, as well as personal, development. I also thank my husband, Rick Kane, who has lived with me, creating our new and different kind of family, for a quarter of a century. And finally I thank our daughter, Leah KaneRisman, whose very existence constantly reminds me why this work that I do is so important. Her presence in my everyday life reminds me that the world is full of joy as well as struggle.

Gender Vertigo

1
Introduction

ender, women, men, sexism, inequality, sex roles, feminism—these topics have received an overwhelming amount of academic and popular attention in the past twenty years. But perhaps most startling is the rapid growth of serious research in these areas. As recently as 1975, when I was taking an undergraduate sociology of deviance course, I was discouraged from writing a paper on rape "because there was nothing in the literature to read about." Today, schools offer entire courses on the topic.

Much contemporary study of gender relations is based implicitly or explicitly on the belief that men and women act differently because girls and boys are raised to be different kinds of creatures. Little girls are still dressed to be adorable—in shiny shoes and easy-to-ruin dresses—and boys are dressed for rough-and-tumble play. Girls take dance lessons; boys learn karate. Feminist psychoanalysts have taken us beyond this focus on explicit socialization, arguing persuasively that being the same sex as one's primary caretaker (almost always the mother) creates an ability to nurture that is unlikely to develop in boys because their same-sex parent is less involved in their care. Girls have other problems, however, according to this new psychoanalytic tradition. They have difficulty creating a separate sense of self—knowing their "boundaries"—because they are so emotionally connected to their mothers. Boys individuate more successfully and go on to develop autonomous self-identities.

But boys have repressed the connection to their mother and, as a result, often have problems with intimacy in relationships.

Although these insights about early childhood socialization and parenting are important, a growing body of research suggests that socialization and gendered personality development do not sufficiently explain gender differences and sexual inequality (Risman and Schwartz 1989). One problem is that such theories usually assume a continuity of behavioral styles and personality preferences throughout life, an assumption challenged by some researchers (Risman 1987; Gerson 1985, 1993; Bielby and Bielby 1984). An even more serious challenge to the socialization theory and to psychoanalytic theorists' attention to the internalization of masculinity and femininity is that the same person may display passive and subordinate "femininity" in a love affair yet be a tyrant at the office. Individuals not only change over their lifetimes, they also can change from moment to moment.

Currently, gender is a taken-for-granted means of organizing all aspects of our society, including our families. Bem (1993) shows that we often reproduce inequality, even when we consciously reject sexism, by continuing to use "lenses of gender" based on hidden assumptions. Bem identifies how three of these hidden assumptions produce the meaning and salience of gender in our society: essentialism, androcentrism, and gender polarization. Essentialism is the assumption that basic differences in orientation and personality between men and women are rooted in biology and nature. Androcentrism is defined as male-centeredness; it is not only the belief that males are more valuable than females but also the more subtle ideology that male experience is somehow gender-neutral and normative for all people. Gender polarization is the assumption that not only are women and men different, but that this difference is "super-imposed on so many aspects of the social world that a cultural connection is thereby forged between sex and virtually every other aspect of human experience, including modes of dress and social roles and even ways of expressing emotion and experiencing sexual desire" (2). Bem argues persuasively that one cannot justify androcentrism or essentialism without gender polarization. And she shows us how gender polarization (or vast and dichotomous differences between biological males and females) is socially constructed at the psychological and cultural levels.

I have spent the past decade trying to understand why men and women behave so differently, particularly in their intimate relationships. I came of age during the height of feminist activism in the United States, and as a college student I threw myself into the movement. But I was also deeply involved in my training as a sociologist, becoming increasingly aware that activists must understand why people behave as they do before we can solve social problems. As a fledgling sociologist, I knew that we must identify the processes that cause people to behave as they do. It is to that task that I turned, first as a graduate student and now as a teacher, researcher, and activist. It remains my intellectual preoccupation.

In this book I integrate and present work that is a culmination of thinking and research—my own and others'—since I began graduate school in 1976. I introduce a new conceptual language to help explain exactly what "gender" means and how it comes to exist and to be reproduced. This book is about how and why women and men make choices about, adapt to, and sometimes change the conditions that profoundly affect their most intimate relationships—as partners and parents. I suggest that gender is itself a social structure. Just as the economy is central to our lives, gender organizes our world. But the gender structure, unlike the economic or political structure, seems so "natural" and is so accepted that we seldom even see it.

Although most structural analyses focus on how structures create behavior—constraining it or making it possible—the role of human beings in creating or producing social structures is integral to any multilevel structural theory of gender (Lorber 1994). In this book I outline a theory that addresses both the continued existence of gender as a structural aspect of society and the efforts of some feminists to make it irrelevant to the distribution of rights and responsibilities—that is, to create a society without gender as a social structure.

I focus on the contemporary heterosexual family not because gender is more pervasive here than elsewhere or because the family is a more important institution than any other but rather because the family is the one institution in which we are all produced and in which many of us display—day by day—our gender. Berk (1985) characterizes the family as a gender factory in which gender polarization is both made and displayed. For example, perhaps the best explanation for why women traditionally do so much more household labor than men do is that society has defined such work as part of "being" a woman and appropriately "doing gender" (West and Zimmerman 1987). It is perhaps in the family and other intimate relationships that gender is still accepted, even ideologically, as a reasonable and legitimate basis for the distribution of rights, power, privilege, and responsibilities. It is at home that most people come to believe that men and women are and should be essentially different.

But most of the families that I discuss in this book are at the margins of traditional gender expectations in the United States. I look at test cases, people living in nontraditional configurations, in order to challenge the dominant individualist model that women and men approach their families differently because of their gendered personalities. These kinds of families—single fathers, for instance, and feminist couples—have to swim against the current, and I watch what happens to them and to our society as they take on this task. When I turn my attention to more traditional families I find a statistical and shrinking minority: married mothers who have some choice about whether to work for pay. Therefore, I must be emphatic about the lack of representativeness of the families discussed in this book: these families are, by design, atypical.

I focus on the hierarchical nature of gender structure. Just as "separate but equal" is impossible to achieve in race relations, I believe that separate spheres of responsibility are inherently unequal in contemporary gender relations. Simply accepting gender as a legitimate basis for any role allocation validates inequality (West and Zimmerman 1987; Lorber 1994). Although some foraging societies may have had both a gender-based division of labor and near equality of men and women (e.g., Chafetz 1984), such a scenario is unlikely in a post-industrial society, where ideology dictates that social position be based on achievement. This principle of meritocracy underlies our competitive educational system and hiring practices. The logic of meritocracy contradicts the logic of ascription, yet one's sex category (whether one is considered male or female) is nearly always ascribed. To the extent that such ascriptive status determines behavioral norms, constraints, and opportunities, inequality is inevitable. The very existence of a gender structure legitimates the organization of social life based on the ascribed category of sex and therefore legitimates inequality.

But does my argument mean that we are doomed to re-create gender inequality forever, whether we want to or not? Is gender so integral to human social organization that we cannot overcome it? No. *Gender structure* organizes our lives, usually in ways that support the status quo. But the theory and research evidence offered here suggest that actors shape the gender structure they inherit. Although no social structure can be ignored, we are not robots. Our predecessors created our social structure, but we can and do change it all the time.

My argument builds directly on the work of theorists who define gender as a stratification system based on categorization created and reinforced every day (Bem 1993; Ferree and Hess 1987; Ferree 1990; West and Zimmerman 1987; Risman and Schwartz 1989; Lorber 1994). Gender theorists do not assume that dichotomous gender categories or sex-based social roles are "natural," even in families. Nor do gender theorists assume that gender boundaries are or should be stable. My work also builds on the theoretical groundwork of those who have brought structural analysis to gender theory (Lerner 1986; Acker 1992; Connell 1987; Lorber 1994; O'Brien 1983; Sprague 1988, 1991; Mies 1986). I move beyond that work by arguing that we must conceptualize *gender* as a *structure,* with ideological and material components that affect social life at every level of analysis.[1]

The thesis that I offer in this book is that gender structure on the interactional level bears heavy responsibility for continuing gender inequality in American family life. I believe that the expectations we face each day—the opportunities and constraints we negotiate as we interact with one another—are much to blame for the male privileges still accorded in contemporary American families. The consequences of the gender structure for individuals and for economic and political institutions matter. We are unequivocally taught to be feminine women and masculine men. And nearly every organization is built on gendered principles. But these are not the only or even the most important reasons that adults follow gendered scripts in their most intimate relationships. We also "do gender"— follow the rules and behaviors expected of us, because if we don't, we are judged immoral and incompetent as men and women. But

---

1. Lorber (1994) argues that gender should be defined as an "institution," with much the same definition that I use for the term "structure." While I build on her analysis, I prefer the term "structure" because my work also builds directly on structural sociological theory.

doing gender means creating differences that are not inevitable or essential. And when we do gender we re-create the expectation that men and women not only do but ought to behave differently. For example, when a man holds a door open for a woman, his conscious motivation may simply be to behave politely. But if that woman is his colleague, he has differentiated her from himself, treated her more as a female rather than by any other criterion (boss, work partner, even work subordinate). He has re-created and supported a system of meanings in which she is woman before all else. This supports the status quo, intentionally or not. We are all free, of course, to do gender or not. But "free choices" are made within social constraints, and nonconformity often involves great personal sacrifice. We can choose only from options that exist, in fact or at least in imagination.

There is good evidence that when economic and institutional barriers to equality are dismantled, families do indeed become more egalitarian. And yet economic and institutional changes do not eradicate gender polarization. In Sweden, where parental leave and part-time work are available for all parents of young children, fathers are more involved in child care than in the United States. But they are still not as involved as mothers (Haas 1992). Similarly, in Israeli kibbutzim, child care was socialized and mothers were full participants in economic labor. And yet child care remained women's work and power remained in men's hands (Blumberg 1986; Hazleton 1977; Agassi 1989). In the former Soviet Union, maternal leave and child care was available to all — to all women, that is — because gender itself was never problematized (see Corrin 1993 and Funk and Mueller 1993). In each of these societies gender expectations remained even when economic and political institutions began to accommodate women's expanding roles, and gender continued to organize social life. I suggest that until we problematize the very meaning of gender and how it affects our interactions in families, we can never imagine a world without it framing our choices.

In Chapter 2, I analyze what it means to define gender as a social structure, and I focus on the importance of the interactional expectations that are part of the structural contexts and work to support hierarchical gender relations in families. I explain why gender stratification exists. I argue that we must conceptualize gender itself as a structure with consequences at the individual, interactional, and institutional levels. I critique how gender has been conceptualized historically, within both family sociology and the general study of intimate relationships. I then offer my own conceptual analysis, focusing on the hierarchical nature of gender relations in families. I illustrate my arguments with a story about a hypothetical feminist couple.

In Chapters 3, 4, and 5, I discuss my own and others' research on relationships between parents and children and between husbands and wives. Chapter 3 is based primarily on a survey I conducted of 220 families—55 headed by employed fathers with stay-at-home mothers, 55 by two employed parents, 55 by single mothers, and 55 by single fathers (Risman 1987). I use these data to ask the questions, "Can men mother? Are men capable of doing women's work, mothering, when they have to?" Much research has shown that when women enter the labor force and are given opportunities equal to those ordinarily given to men, they excel despite their sex-role socialization. Until now, however, the question of whether our society can trust men to do well at the vital work of nurturing the next generation has not really been answered. Women are clearly competent workers, but can men "mother" children? And if they cannot, what does that mean for women? And for the possibility of sexual equality? My argument and my data suggest that men are capable "mothers" but that currently most men do mothering work only when they do not have wives to do it for them.

In Chapter 4, I focus on marital relationships, asking how women make choices about their lives. How can we predict or explain which women will remain committed to paid work, even when married, and which will become domestic wives? The theoretical issue here is central to my theory of gender. Are some women so well socialized to desire and expect traditional lives that they consciously and effectively choose domestic work as their career? Or do women's choices hinge less on their socialized femininity than on their failures and successes in the labor force or their husband's characteristics? Why do some women retain their economic independence and others depend exclusively on their husbands for their own and their children's economic survival? I rely primarily on research conducted by my colleagues and me (Risman, Atkinson, and Blackwelder 1994). We analyzed data that tracked women's career and family plans from the time they were juniors or seniors in high school in 1966 until they were in their early thirties, in 1979. The women in this study are nearly all white, raised when traditional expectations reigned supreme—when white girls were raised to become mothers and wives. Yet this is also the generation who lived through the rebirth of the feminist movement and entered the labor force in droves. We test the strength of an individual woman's sex-role socialization versus the constraints and opportunities in her adult work and family life as alternative explanations for the level of her participation in the labor force as an adult. Our data suggest, as does the theory offered here, that the structural conditions of adult life far outweigh sex-role training as the explanation for women's life trajectories.

In Chapter 5, I present findings from a collaborative study (with Stephen Blackwelder, Sandra Godwin, Steven Jolly, Kristin Myers, Jammie Price, Margaret Stiffler, and Danette Johnson-Sumerford) of fifteen feminist families. We have been intensively interviewing and then observing (in their own homes) families who are "fair," in which the husband and wife—and our quantitative survey instrument—actually agree that they are equally responsible for earning the family wage and doing the family labor of housework and childrearing. Our study is unique because we not only interviewed and observed both parents but also included the children in our research. We ask how women and men living in a gender-stratified society have managed to overcome a gender-based division of family labor. But we also explore the consequences for children living in such homes. Do the children conceptualize gender differently from their peers? Or does their own egalitarian family pale in comparison to the gender structured world they see everywhere else they look? We analyze data from children as young as four to those finishing high school. I discuss what aspects of contemporary gender structures have changed to allow these families to renegotiate their lives, and I speculate on the effects such families might have on our society.

I hope that the data presented will demonstrate that gender is not merely internalized into us as masculine and feminine personalities. Rather, the pervasive differences between male and female styles in personal relationships are continuously created by the gender structures in which we all live. The research reported suggests that the gender structure endures in families not only or even primarily because we socialize children for compliance, but because we organize the interactional contexts so that doing gender is usually the easiest means to thrive, or even survive, in our society. And when that rare context emerges that supports gender-atypical behaviors, we see that it is indeed possible to do it differently.

In the final chapter I deal with the implications of my structural analysis for feminist social change. I argue the quite radical position that we must go beyond gender as a category for organizing our families and our public world. (See Bem 1993 for an earlier formulation of this argument.) I suggest that we start by going beyond gender whenever we can, ignoring gendered rules, pushing the envelope until we get dizzy. Gender vertigo can only help us to destabilize deeply held but incorrect beliefs about the natural differences between women and men. I believe that we will have to be dizzy for a time if we are to hope to deconstruct gender and construct a society based on equality. I argue that as long as behavioral expectations, material advantages, and cultural ideology divide human beings into types based on their ascribed sex (that is, the shape of their genitals), male privilege will continue. I end with some suggestions for how to begin to separate gender from ourselves, our families, and our world. For I firmly believe that only when gender becomes no more important than the color of our eyes will biological females attain equality in a post-industrial twenty-first century.

I cannot end this introduction without a caveat. This book is not merely sociological theory and research but sociology *for* women, not of women or even simply of gender relations. My science aims to improve the status of women in a society in which men have much greater access to power, property, and prestige. I am interested in identifying the processes most important for constructing gender, because we must understand how a category is created before we can deconstruct it. Through this work I hope to contribute to the monumental task of empowering women.

I am, however, painfully aware that not all men are equally privileged or fully empowered in our society. It is beyond argument that women in privileged economic settings have more access to societal rewards than do men born into underprivileged families. But it is also true that in every community in our society men have more privilege and status than their sisters or mothers do. In this work, I focus exclusively on how gender is constructed. Clearly, however, gender is constructed interlocking with other social structures and within a matrix of domination (Collins 1991). I hope and believe that my theory could just as well be applied to other socially constructed categories of difference on which we base stratification systems. And I believe that further applications or extensions of this theory will help us explore how the various axes on which we base social inequality (race, ethnicity, sexuality) intersect with gender. My work is an attempt to build a theory that looks carefully at how *gender as a social structure* affects our everyday interactions. While the content of such interactions clearly differs in each cultural and ethnic community, gendered interaction is ubiquitous.

2
Gender as Structure

There are three distinct theoretical traditions that help us to understand sex and gender, and a fourth is now taking shape. The first tradition focuses on gendered selves, whether sex differences are biological or social in origin. The second tradition, which emerged as a reaction to the first, focuses on how the social structure (as opposed to biology or individual learning) creates gendered behavior. The third tradition, also a reaction to the individualist thinking of the first, emphasizes contextual issues and how doing gender re-creates inequality during interaction. The fourth, multilevel approach treats gender itself as built in to social life via socialization, interaction, and institutional organization. This new perspective integrates the previous ones; it is formed on the assumption that each viewpoint sheds different light on the same question. This book contributes to this developing integrative and multilevel perspective.

Gendered Selves

There are numerous theoretical perspectives within this tradition, but all share the assumption that maleness and femaleness are, or become, properties of individuals. That is why I see this as an individualist approach. Research questions in this tradition focus on the development of sex differences and their relative importance for behavior.

The "natural" difference argument gained renewed interest with the development of sociobiology (e.g., Wilson 1975 and Van den

Berghe 1979) and biosociology (Rossi 1977, 1984). Sociobiologists have argued that such behaviors as male aggressiveness and female nurturance result from natural selection. Biosociologists stress the infant care skills in which females appear to excel. Their perspective has been criticized for its ethnocentrism and its selective use of biological species as evidence (see Epstein 1988).

More recent biosocial theories have posited complex interactions between environment and biological predispositions, with attention to explaining intrasex differences. This new version of biosociology may eventually help to identify the biological parameters that, in interaction with environmental stimuli, affect human behavior. An interesting example of such work is Booth and Dabbs' (1992) research linking high testosterone levels in men with poor marriages. But the researchers hypothesize that the relation between testosterone levels and marital quality may manifest itself only—or more strongly—among certain males, particularly those without a strong internal locus of control. Thus, they suggest a complex interaction between the social and the biological.

Sex-role socialization theorists explain the differences between men's and women's behavior in intimate relationships by relying not on "nature" but on more sophisticated ideas. Connell (1987) suggests that the shift from biological assumptions allowed theorists to address the connections between social structure and the formation of personality. A voluminous literature developed on agencies of socialization, particularly the family. Sex role theory suggests that early childhood socialization is an influential determinant of later behavior, and research has focused on how societies create feminine women and masculine men.

There is an impressive variety of sex-role explanations for gender-differentiated behavior in families. Perhaps the most commonly accepted explanation is reinforcement theory (e.g., Bandura and Walters 1963, Mischel 1966, and Weitzman 1979). Reinforcement theory suggests, for example, that girls develop nurturant personalities because they are given praise and attention for their interest in dolls and babies, and that boys develop competitive selves because they are positively reinforced for winning, whether at checkers or football. Although much literature suggests that the socialization experiences of boys and girls continue to differ dramatically, it is clearly the case that most girls raised in the 1990s have received ambiguous gender socialization: they have been taught to desire domesticity (dolls remain a popular toy for girls), as well as to pursue careers. For generations, African American girls have been socialized both for motherhood and paid work (Collins 1990).

Nancy Chodorow's (1978, 1989) feminist psychoanalytic analysis approach has also been influential, particularly in feminist scholarship. Chodorow develops an object-relations psychoanalytic perspective to explain how gendered personalities develop as a result of exclusively female mothering. She focuses on how the relationship between infant and mother, in the pre-oedipal period, shapes feminine and masculine personalities. Chodorow notices, as did Freud (1933) and Parsons (1954), that mothers are responsible for young children almost universally. She argues that mothers relate to their boy and girl infants differently, fusing identities with their daughters while relating to their sons as separate and distinct. As a result, according to this feminist version of psychoanalysis, girls develop selves based on connectedness and relationships while boys develop selves based on independence and autonomy. In addition, boys must reject their first love-object (mother) in order to adopt masculinity, and they do this by rejecting and devaluing what is feminine in themselves and in society. Thus, we get nurturant women and independent men in a society dominated by men and which values independence. Many feminist studies have incorporated this psychoanalytic view of gender as an underlying assumption (L. Rubin 1982; Keller 1985; Williams 1989).

Just as psychoanalytic thought has influenced feminist scholarship, feminist theorizing about differences (Collins 1990) has influenced psychoanalytic theorizing. Chodorow (1994) has pushed her theoretical stance to incorporate the differences between women and between men by looking at how American families differ ethnically; she even speculates with cross-historical and international comparisons.

Other feminist theorists, such as Ruddick (1989, 1992) and Aptheker (1989), build on the notion that the constant nature of mothering creates a certain kind of thinking, what Ruddick calls "maternal thinking." The logic of this argument does not depend on a psychoanalytic framework, but it implicitly uses one: through nurturing their children women develop psychological frameworks that value peace and justice. Therefore, if women (or men who mothered children) were powerful political actors, governments would use more peaceful conflict resolution strategies and value social justice more highly.

All individualist theories, including sex-role socialization and psychoanalytic thought, posit that by adulthood most men and women have developed very different personalities. Women have become nurturant, person oriented, and child centered. Men have become competitive and work oriented. According to individualist theorists, there are limits to flexibility. Intensely held emotions, values, and inclinations developed during childhood coalesce into a person's self-identity. Although these theorists do not deny that social structures influence family patterns, nor that notions of gender meaning are always evolving (see especially Chodorow 1995), they focus on how culturally determined family patterns and sex-role socialization create gendered selves, which then provide the motivations for individuals to fill their socially appropriate roles.

Historically, sex-role theorists have assumed that men and women behave differently because gender resides primarily in personality. This approach has several serious conceptual weaknesses (for detailed analyses of such problems, see Connell 1987 and Ferree 1990). First, such theories usually presume behavioral continuity throughout the life course. In fact, women socialized for nurturance are capable of competitive and aggressive behavior, and men raised without any expectation of taking on primary responsibility can "mother" when they need to (Risman 1987; Gerson 1985, 1993; Bielby and Bielby 1984). Another weakness of these individualist-oriented theories is their oversocialized conception of human behavior—that once we know how an individual has been raised, the training is contained primarily inside his or her head (cf. Wrong 1961). Such theories might suggest, for example, that women do not revolt and are not necessarily unhappy with their subordinate status because they have been so well trained for femininity. While the development of gendered selves is clearly an important predictor of gender differences in adult relationships, Thorne's (1993) research shows dramatically the variability in developmental experiences of boys and girls.

This overdependence on internalization of culture and socialization leads to the most serious problem with sex-role theory: its depoliticization of gender inequality. Although sex-role socialization and revisionist psychoanalytic theorists often have explicitly feminist goals, their focus on sex differences has legitimated a dualistic conception of gender that relies on a reified male/female dichotomy. The very notion of comparing all men to all women without regard for diversity within groups presumes that gender is primarily about individual differences between biological males and biological females, downplaying the role of interactional expectations and the social structure.

The sex-role socialization theory is an application of a normative role theory for human behavior. It assumes that social stability is motivated primarily by beliefs and values acquired during socialization. Individuals are assumed to use whatever resources are available to realize these values and to maintain their identities. As Stokes and Hewitt (1976) have argued, socialization cannot serve as the fundamental link between culture and action. Indeed, studies of intergenerational shifts in values suggest that economic and political conditions produce beliefs, attitudes, and preferences for action that overcome those acquired during childhood (Lesthaeghe 1980; Inglehart 1977, 1981). We cannot assume that internalization of norms — through psychoanalytic processes or sex-role socialization — is the primary means by which society organizes human conduct.

In her review of findings based on meta-analytic research,[1] Eagly (1995) suggests that psychologists who study sex differences have reached a new consensus: empirical research does indeed support the existence of certain sex differences, and it confirms that many assumed differences are more myth than reality. Empirical analyses

---

1. It used to be that studies were synthesized and conclusions were drawn rather informally. In reviews of sex differences, for example, studies were dichotomized, with the number of those that found statistically significant differences balanced against those that did not. Often results were mixed and conclusions hard to draw. An even bigger problem was that the quality of the studies was not assessed, so that several studies that were methodologically weak might be considered more weighty than one very strong study. The most famous and influential of these reviews was by Maccoby and Jacklin (1974). In the new meta-analytic techniques, more information about each study is identified and coded quantitatively. The size of the sex difference, as well as the quality of the research methodology (including measures for central tendency of the effect sizes, distribution, measurement validity and reliability, and internal consistency), can all be incorporated into decisions about which sex differences actually exist in the sample population. Computer analyses weight variables and identify which differences exist based on the strongest methodologies. Although this quantitative review technique cannot overcome major limitations in the quality of the studies assessed, it does offer substantial gains over reviews that use a more impressionistic reading of the literature.

consistently find differences in quantitative problem solving among adolescents and adults, differences in visual spatial ability, and differences in verbal fluency. Some nontrivial differences in aspects of social interaction and personality are reported. "The question of *whether* sex differences exist has evolved into the more demanding question of *why* the sexes differ considerably at some times and at other times differ moderately, minimally, or not at all" (Eagly 1995, 13). *Why* has become the question among psychologists; it is their question and mine.

Structure vs. Personality

The overreliance on gendered selves as the primary explanation for sexual stratification led many feminist sociologists—myself included—to argue that what appear to be sex differences are really, in Epstein's terms, "deceptive distinctions" (Epstein 1988; Kanter 1977; Risman and Schwartz 1989). Although empirically documented sex differences do occur, structuralists like me have argued that men and women behave differently because they fill different positions in institutional settings, work organizations, or families. That is, the previous structural perspectives on gender assume that work and family structures create empirically distinct male and female behavior. Structuralist feminist sociologists (e.g., Kanter 1976, Risman 1987, Risman and Schwartz 1989, and Epstein 1988) have not usually conceptualized gender itself as a structure. Rather, most have argued that empirically documented sex differences are more apparent than real. Within this perspective, men and women in the same structural slots are expected to behave identically. Epstein's (1988) voluminous review of the multidisciplinary research on gender and sex differences is perhaps the strongest and most explicit support for a social-structural explanation of gendered behavior. She suggests that there are perhaps no empirically documented differences that can be traced to the predispositions of males and females. Instead, the deceptive differences reflect women's lack of opportunity in a male-dominated society.

Gender relations in the labor force have received far more of this sort of structural analysis than have gender relations in intimate settings. Kanter's classic work *Men and Women of the Corporation* (1977) introduced this kind of structural perspective on gender in the workplace. Kanter showed that when women had access to powerful mentors, interactions with people like themselves, and the possibility for upward mobility, they behaved like others — regardless of sex — with similar advantages. These social network variables could explain success at work far better than could assumptions of masculine versus feminine work styles. Women were less often successful because they were more often blocked from network advantages, not because they feared success or had never developed competitive strategies. Men who lacked such opportunities did not advance, and they behaved with stereotypical feminine work styles. Kanter argued persuasively that structural system properties better explain sex differences in workplace behavior than does sex-role socialization.

A large body of research has been built on Kanter's ideas concerning apparent gender differences and actual inequality in the labor force (e.g., Thompson 1981, Rosenfield 1979, Lorber 1984, Baron and Bielby 1985, and Geis et al. 1984). This focus on structural inequities in gender relations has become a mainstream perspective in sociological studies of women in the work force (Reskin 1989).

The application of a structural perspective to gender within personal relationships has been less frequent, but at least two explicit attempts have been made. In a series of studies (Risman 1986, 1987, 1988), I tested whether apparent sex differences in parenting styles are better attributed to sex-role socialization or to the structural contingencies of adult life. The question I asked was "Can men mother?" The answer is yes, but only if they do not have women to do it for them. The lack of sex-role socialization for nurturance did not inhibit the development of male mothering when structural contingencies demanded it. This is an important part of the story, but not all of it.

Gerson's qualitative research (1985, 1993) also provides strong support for a structural theory of gender (she uses the term "developmental" rather than structural). On the basis of retrospective interview data, Gerson reports that half her sample of baby-boom women changed their orientation between domesticity and commitment to work (in both directions) from young adulthood to their early thirties. Gerson suggests that four variables explain the change in orientation: marital stability, the perceived sufficiency of the husband's wage, women's opportunities and experiences in the labor force, and the existence of support networks for domestic wives. Adolescent plans and sex-role socialization did not predict adult choices. Gerson provides similar evidence about men's choices: plans made in adolescence were not accurate predictors of men's family involvement. Labor force experiences and marital stability were better explanations for men's family lives than were their hopes or dreams based on gender socialization.

While applications of structural perspectives both to workplaces and to intimate relationships have furthered the sociological understanding of gender, there is a fundamental flaw in the logic of these arguments. I have claimed elsewhere, as did Kanter a decade before, that if women and men were to experience identical structural conditions and roles expectations, empirically observable gender differences would dissipate. It seemed to me then that gender would nearly disappear when external structural conditions and roles converge for women and men; that is, when structure rather than socialization creates behavior. Now I believe that this is accurate only if we realize that gender itself is a structure deeply embedded in our society.

Research findings led to my reassessment of gender-neutral structural theories: several studies (Williams 1992; Yoder 1991; Zimmer 1988) found that Kanter's hypotheses about the explanatory power of social structural variables such as relative numbers, access to mentors, and upward mobility are not, in fact, gender neutral. That is, Kanter's hypotheses are supported empirically only when societally devalued groups enter traditionally white male work environments. When white males enter traditionally female work environments, they do not hit the glass ceiling, they ride glass elevators. Reskin (1988) has suggested that we have so accepted these "structural" arguments that we sometimes forget that sexism itself stratifies our labor force. Evidence similarly points to continued existence of gendered behavior in family settings. Hertz reported that in her 1986 study of couples in which husbands and wives hold equivalent, high-status corporate jobs and brought similar resources to their marriages, the wives continue to shoulder more responsibility for family work (even if that means hiring and supervising help). Despite the importance of structural variables in explaining behavior in families, the sex category itself remains a powerful predictor of who does what kind of family work (Brines 1994; South and Spitz 1994). Gender stratification remains even when other structural aspects of work or of family life are divorced from sex category. The interactionist theory discussed below helps us to understand why.

Doing Gender

This approach to gender was best articulated by West and Zimmerman in their 1987 article "Doing Gender." I believe that they too were reacting to the overdeterminative nature of the sex-differences approach. West and Zimmerman suggest that once a person

is labeled a member of a sex category, she or he is morally accountable for behaving as persons in that category do. That is, the person
is expected to "do gender"; the ease of interaction depends on it.
One of the groundbreaking aspects in this argument is that doing
gender implies legitimating inequality. The authors suggest that,
by definition, what is female in a patriarchal society is devalued.
Within this theoretical framework, the very belief that biological
males and females are essentially different (apart from their repro-
ductive capabilities) exists to justify male dominance.

The tradition of doing gender has been well accepted in feminist sociology (West and Zimmerman's article was cited in jour-
nals more than one hundred times by 1995). West and Zimmerman
articulated an insight whose time had come—that gender is not
what we are but something that we do. Psychologists Deaux and
Major (1990) use similarly interactional theories to explain gender.
They argue that much of the literature on sex difference is inaccurate because it measures behavior but pays no attention to interaction. They suggest that interactional contexts take priority over
individual traits and personality differences; others' expectations
create the self-fulfilling prophecies that lead all of us to do gender. Deaux and Major go beyond simply endorsing an interactional
theory, however. They suggest that actual behavior depends on
the interaction of participants' self-definitions, the expectations of
others, and the cultural expectations attached to the context itself. I
agree. The weakness in the doing gender approach is that it under-
theorizes the pervasiveness of gender inequality in organizations
and gendered identities.

Although gender is always present in our interaction, it is not
present only in interaction. We must have a theoretical link from
material constraints to what we do now, to who we think we are. I
suggest that the doing-gender perspective is incomplete because it
slights the institutional level of analysis and the links among institu-

tional gender stratification, situational expectations, and gendered selves.

West and Fenstermaker (1995) have extended the argument from doing gender to "doing difference." They suggest that just as we create inequality when we create gender during interaction, so we create race and class inequalities when we interact in daily life. Race does not generally hold the biologically based assumption of dichotomy (as sex category does), yet in American society we constantly use race categories to guide our interactional encounters. This extension of theoretical ideas from gender to the analysis of inequalities is perhaps the most important direction gender theorizing has taken in the past decade. Black feminist thought (see particularly Brewer 1989, P. Collins 1990, hooks 1984, and King 1988) has sensitized many white feminists to the notion that theories of "women" have often assumed that middle-class white women represent the entire category. As I describe the emerging perspective within which I work, I want to stress that even though gender is a structure in every context, the actual content can vary dramatically. What does not vary is that gender is the basis for sexual stratification (Lorber 1994).

Gender as Social Structure

The sex-differences literature, the doing-gender contextual analyses, and the structural perspectives are not necessarily incompatible, although I, as well as others, have portrayed them as alternatives (e.g., Kanter 1977, Epstein 1988, Risman 1987, Risman and Schwartz 1989, and Ferree 1990). More recently, England and Browne (1992) argued persuasively that every sociological theory makes implicit assumptions about internalized states and external social control. Chodorow also argues (1995) that we must study gender as both a personal and cultural construction; the psyche can deal only with material experienced in our world as it is currently structured. While most structural theories focus only on external social constraint, I follow England and Browne's (1992) argument that all external constraints eventually affect selves; my empirical question is after how long and with what force. I am also convinced by Chodorow's argument (1995) that we must attend to individual selves—and gender meaning at this level—because individuals choose to make social change. My view of gender as a social structure incorporates each level of analysis, even if my major focus here is more narrow.

Lorber (1994) argues that gender is an entity in and of itself that establishes patterns of expectations for individuals, orders social processes of everyday life, and is built into all other major social organizations of society. She goes further, however, to argue that gender difference is *primarily* a means to justify sexual stratification. Gender is so ubiquitous because unless we see difference, we cannot justify inequality. Lorber provides much cross-cultural, literary, and scientific evidence to show that gender difference is socially constructed and yet is universally used to justify stratification. She writes that "the continuing purpose of gender as a modern social institution is to construct women as a group to be subordinate to men as a group" (33).

I build on this notion that gender is an entity in and of itself and has consequences at every level of analysis. And I share the concern that the very creation of difference is the foundation on which inequality rests. In my view, it is most useful to conceptualize gender as a structure that has consequences for every aspect of society. And while the language of structure suits my purposes better than any other, it is not ideal. Despite its ubiquity in sociological discourse, no definition of the term "structure" is widely shared (see Smelser 1988 for a review of various structural traditions). So I begin by explaining what I mean by structure and how I have derived my definition. Some consensus exists. All structuralists presume that social structures exist outside individual desires or motives and that the structures can at least partially explain human action. All structural theorists would agree that social structure constrains human action or makes it possible.

Blau's (1977) now classic definition of social structure focused solely on the constraint that collective life imposes on the individual. In their influential work, Blau and his colleagues (e.g., Rytina et al. 1988) have argued that the concept of structure is trivialized if it is located inside an individual's head in the form of internalized norms and values. Structure must be conceptualized, in this view, as a force opposing individual motivation. Structural concepts must be observable, external to the individual, and independent of individual motivation. This definition of structure imposes a clear dualism between structure and action, with structure as constraint and action as choice. I incorporate Blau's analysis of structure as constraint, but I reject the notion that structure constrains action only externally.

In order to analyze human action, we must understand not only how the social structure acts as constraint but also how and why actors choose one alternative over another. Burt (1982) suggests that actors compare themselves and their options to those in structurally similar positions. In this view, actors are purposive, rationally seeking to maximize their self-perceived well-being under social structural constraints.[2] Actions are a function of interests, but interests and ability to choose are patterned by the social structure. Burt suggests that norms develop when actors occupying similar network positions in the social structure evaluate their own options

---

2. Burt's notion of purposive and rational action differs from that of more atomistic theorists because he does not assume that actors necessarily have enough information to act effectively in their own best interest. Nor does he assume that the consequences of actions are necessarily intended.

vis-à-vis the alternatives of similarly situated others. From such comparisons evolve both norms and feelings of relative deprivation or advantage. The social structure as the context of daily life creates action indirectly by shaping actors' perceptions of their interests and directly by constraining choice.

Giddens' (1984) theory adds considerable depth to the analysis of social structures as existing in a recursive relationship to individuals. That is, social structures shape individuals even as individuals are shaping their social structure. Giddens rejects a structuralism (e.g., Blau 1977) that ignores the transformative power of human action. He insists that any structural theory must be concerned with reflexivity and actors' interpretations of their own lives. When people act on structure, they do so for their own reasons. We must, therefore, be concerned with why people act as they do. Giddens insists that this concern go beyond the verbal justification easily available from actors because much of social life is so routine that actors will not articulate, or even consider, why they act. Giddens refers to this reality as practical consciousness. I refer to it as the cultural aspect of the social structure: the taken-for-granted or cognitive image rules that belong to the situational context (not only or necessarily to the actor's personality). Within this framework, we must pay considerable attention to how structure makes action possible as well as constrains it. We must bring individuals back into structural theories.

Connell (1987) applies Giddens' theory of social structure as both constraint and as created by action in his treatise on gender and power (see particularly chap. 5).[3] In his analysis, structure is assumed to specify what constrains action, and yet "since human action involves free invention . . . and is reflexive, practice can be

---

3. Connell refers to action as "practice."

turned against what constrains it; so structure can deliberately be the object of practice" (95). Action may turn against structure, but it can never escape it. An accurate analysis of any hierarchical relationship requires a focus both on how structure shapes interaction and on how human agency creates structure (Blackwelder 1993). A multilevel theory of gender as a social structure must acknowledge causality as recursive—action itself may change the immediate or future context. I build on Connell's analysis of the reflexivity of action and structure, although I return to that argument primarily in the last chapter.

Gender itself must be considered a structural property of society. It is not manifested just in our personalities, our cultural rules, or other institutions. Gender is deeply embedded as a basis for stratification, differentiating opportunities and constraints. This differentiation has consequences on three levels: (1) at the individual level, for the development of gendered selves; (2) at the interactional level, for men and women face different expectations even when they fill the identical structural position; and (3) at the institutional level, for rarely will women and men be given identical positions. Differentiation at the institutional level is based on explicit regulations or laws regarding resource distribution, whether resources be defined as access to opportunities or actual material goods. (See fig. 2.1 for a schematic summary of the argument thus far.)

While the *gender structure* clearly affects selves, cultural rules, and institutions, far too much explanatory power is presumed to rest in the motivation of gendered selves. We live in a very individualistic society that teaches us to make our own choices and take responsibility for our own actions. What this has meant for theories about gender is that a tremendous amount of energy is spent on trying to understand why women and men "choose" to devote their life energies to such different enterprises. The distinctly sociological contribution to the explanation hasn't had enough at-

Figure 2.1.   Gender as Structure

Gender as structure

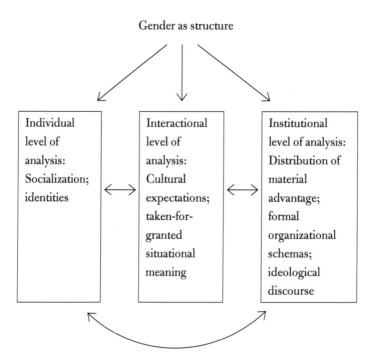

tention: even when individual women and men do *not* desire to live gendered lives or to support male dominance, they often find themselves compelled to do so by the logic of gendered choices. That is, interactional pressures and institutional design create gender and the resultant inequality, even in the absence of individual desires.

My argument and the data presented throughout this book show the strength of our gender structure at the interactional and institutional levels. Choices often assumed to be based on personalities and individual preferences (e.g., consequences of the gender structure at the individual level) are better understood as social constructions based on institutionally constrained opportunities and the limited availability of nongendered cognitive images. Eagly and Woods (1991) offer a useful conceptual scheme for understanding both the continued importance of gender at the individual level and how it differs from an understanding of gender at the contextual level.[4] They suggest that we see individual gendered selves and the cultural expectations of interaction as alternative paths by which gendered institutions influence individual behavior.

Even if individuals are capable of change and wish to eradicate male dominance from their personal lives, the influence of gendered institutions and interactional contexts persists. These contexts are organized by gender stratification at the institutional level, which includes the distribution of material resources organized by gender, the ways by which formal organizations and institutions themselves are gendered, and gendered ideological discourse. For example, in a society in which girls are not taught to read, we could never find a young woman who would be considered a potential international leader. Nor would men denied access to jobs with "family wages" be seen by middle-class American women as good catches for husbands.

At this moment in American society, cultural rules and cognitive images that operate at the interactional level are particularly important in the persistence of gender stratification in families. It is

4. Eagly and Woods do not use the same language I use. I am confident that our conceptual schemes are parallel, and I prefer not to add still more inconsistent language to the text. They describe the institutional level of analysis as the "division of labor between the sexes in society." They use "gender role expectations" for the contextual/interactional level of analysis, and they refer to the individual level of analysis as sex-typed skills and beliefs. They are concerned with explaining empirically identified sex differences in social behavior as dependent variables in psychological research.

not that sex-role socialization or early childhood experience is trivial; gender structure creates gendered selves. But, at this point in history, sex-role socialization itself is ambivalent. In addition, it is clear that even women with feminist worldviews and substantial incomes are constrained by gender structures.

In spite of the removal of some gender discrimination in both law and organizations, gender stratification remains. That is, formal access to opportunities may be gender neutral, yet equality of results may not ensue. Therefore, neither the individual-level explanations nor those based solely on institutional discrimination can explain continued gender stratification in families. Instead, the cognitive images to which we must respond during interaction are the engines that drive continued gender stratification when individuals desire egalitarian relationships and the law allows them (cf. Ridgeway 1997).

Expectations as a Cultural Component of Gender

Handel (1979) and Stokes and Hewitt (1976) provide a framework for integrating structural concerns and interactional theory that helps explain both persistence and change in gender relations. Their work also helps us understand how actors reproduce or contest the gendered contexts in which they find themselves. Handel suggests that normative requirements (e.g., cultural expectations) attached to various roles are inconsistent in modern societies. This "sociological ambivalence" makes it impossible to anticipate precisely the actions of any given person, though we sometimes can anticipate the statistical distributions of action. Individuals view the ambivalent social structure as a problem. Adaptive, situationally negotiated, and emergent conduct is their response. A major interactional task is to confront external structures to which conformity is impossible and to negotiate a situated order. Stokes and Hewitt suggest that culture is not an individualistic trait. Rather, culture is a "learned field of objects that are environmental to action . . . a set of cognitive constraints—objects to which people must relate as they form lines of conduct" (847). Cultural expectations, consistent or ambivalent, become parameters for actions, much like physical constraints and personal history. They allow us to act meaningfully and effectively.

Gender expectations, thus, should be viewed not as internalized masculinity or femininity but as cognitive images (cf. Schwalbe 1987) that constrain action. Cognitive images exist as abstractions, but we have learned them over time both from interaction with others and through cultural images from television, movies, and other media. Every time we do gender we are reacting to cognitive images to which we are accountable, whether we like it or not. People must relate to gender expectations as they decide how to act. Unwritten rules and unspoken beliefs that are part of gender structures can be seen as accurate folklore that must be considered in every interaction. For example, we know that most wives schedule family time, whether or not any given woman actually chooses to do so. And some wives simply expect their husbands to share housework while their husbands view such "help" as a gift. We do not encounter such folklore in the abstract but in the expectations that are part and parcel of relationships. Once we subscribe to such folklore as a moral necessity of being a man or women, then we are motivated to behave morally, to do gender. We become emotionally invested in doing gender, which is one way that we show ourselves and others that we are, indeed, moral actors.

Yet the clarity by which doing gender shows moral worth is clouding as we close the twentieth century. Neither men nor women know when their gender assumptions will be shared by others of the same or opposite sex, even in their immediate social networks. Therefore, constant negotiation and incipient conflict exist even in the most intimate and loving relationships.

Hochschild's (1989) insightful analysis of the emotional distance between husband and wives in dual-earner marriages is a clear example of the consequences of such incipient conflict. Some couples deal with ambivalent gender structure by changing or aligning their actions; others make justifications and give accounts; and some openly rebel. Most dual-earner couples give accounts to help explain their gender "strategies" when their conduct is at odds with their norms. One couple in Hochschild's study portrays this pattern quite creatively by defining the downstairs of their home (which is in reality a garage and playroom) as "half" of their living space, the "half" for which the husband is responsible. Much research suggests that the most typical American couple today professes to believe in gender equality, but the employed wife is still doing a "second shift" — domestic family service.

Neither the individual-level explanations nor those based solely on institutional discrimination can explain continued gender inequality in American families. Right now, the cultural rules and cognitive images explain why actors do gender in ways that support male privilege in family life even when those actors have overcome much internalized oppression and many institutional barriers. The cognitive images to which we must respond during interaction drive continued gender stratification even when individuals desire egalitarian relationships and the law mandates them. Ridgeway (1997) argues that gender stratification is impervious to attempts at social change because sex categorization is an easy solution to the ever-present problem of coordinating human activity. Expectations attached to sex category — accurate or not — provide a cluster of behaviors that we can expect from strangers and that help us to guess how we should behave toward them. Gender is something we do in order to make daily life more manageable. For example, think how hard it would be to share an office with someone whose sex was not obvious to you. The problem, however, is that the differing expectations attached to members of the male and female sex categories are not morally equivalent. Ridgeway argues that they can never be so. Whatever the origins of sexual inequality (and I will not tangle with that question in this book), the expectations of unequal worth are attached to sex category itself. Empirical research (Ridgeway 1997) shows clearly that even in settings in which gender is irrelevant to the task at hand men are presumed to be smarter, more worth listening to, and better leaders. People presumed to be relatively smarter and more worth listening to will have greater impact than others on group decisions—they will become more important. The consequences of gender structure at the interactional level not only reinforce but also re-create inequality even when change might otherwise be possible.

The reconceptualization of gender as a social structure at every level helps us to understand stability and change in contemporary American marriage. Gender rules and cognitive expectations operate as interactional constraints that often create gender hierarchy even among heterosexual feminist couples who bring equivalent external material resources to their relationship. We find that the few heterosexual couples who can repudiate internalized gendered selves and overcome many of the barriers to equality in the workplace still often fail to find equality in marriage. Alternatives are so constrained within our gender structure that even those who consciously reject inequality based on gender may be contributing to the re-creation of gender stratified marriages and to a social structure that disadvantages women. The re-creation of a gender-stratified society is an unintended consequence of institutionally constrained actions—even of those committed to gender equality, and even in a society where laws are at least nominally gender-neutral. Gender structure at the interactional and institutional levels so thoroughly organizes our work, family, and community lives that even those who reject gender inequality in principle sometimes end up being compelled by the "logic" of gendered situations and cognitive images to choose gendered strategies.[5]

I do not mean to suggest that we do not all own gendered selves, or that institutional sexism has disappeared. Rather, I am simply suggesting that even if we overcame our gendered predispositions and were lucky enough to overcome most of the barriers of institutional sexism, the consequences of gender at the interactional level would still constrain our attempts at social change.

Feminist Marriage: Conflict among Images, Institutions, and New Selves

Traditional marriage is male dominated. The very terminology used to describe the husband—"the head of the household"—says it clearly. Yet it would be hard to isolate how gender structure *constrains* individuals when individual ideologies, cultural cognitive images, and the institutional force of law are all consistent and interdependent. The consequences of gender structure at the interactional and institutional levels are most easily illustrated when the structure operates in opposition to internalized normative desires. It is currently possible to analyze the effects of gender structure at the interactional and institutional levels despite individual-level opposition to stratification. That is, it is possible to imagine and locate couples committed to gender equality and to analyze how contextual and institutional levels of gender structure affect them. I argue that our gender structure pushes even committed feminists toward a gendered division of labor and toward male-dominated relationships.

---

5. Choosing the best of bad alternatives is clearly not a free choice at all. Still, I use the language of choice to remind readers that individual actors wrestle with alternatives and make decisions.

On the cultural level, the consequences of gender structure clearly exist beyond the individuals involved. The normative expectations attached to gender in marriage (one aspect of the "rules") are very strong. Gender remains a "master status" (e.g., Hughes 1945), an organizing principle of marriage; expectations imputed to actors nearly always differ by sex. For example, men are not expected to assume a reflective identity (e.g., to become a Mr. Her) upon marriage. Because a reflective identity is based on association with someone else, it is a subordinate identity. Similarly, routine marital rituals are gender stratified. Bridal showers are based on the assumption that women will shoulder the responsibility for domestic labor. Fathers give away brides to the bridegrooms. Not all couples follow these rituals, of course. But when they do not, they are seen as making a choice that requires explanation. No choice is perceived, no explanations are needed, if rituals are followed. Most young couples, at least those without strong ideological commitments, follow the routine path without considering the unintended consequences: creating yet another stratified marriage.

Marriage is only one institution in which gender stratification is manifested, and it may not even be the most oppressive institution, softened as it can be by warm feelings. Yet marriage is one of the linchpins of inequality in American society. In what other institution are social roles, rights, and responsibilities based—even ideologically—on ascribed characteristics? When life options are tied to racial categories we call it racism at best and apartheid at worst. When life options are tied to gender categories we call it marriage.

The social structure clearly constrains gendered action even as it makes it possible. Wives, even those who have no motivation to provide domestic service to their husbands, are constrained to do so by social expectations. A husband who has a disheveled appearance reflects poorly on his wife's domestic abilities (in real life as well as "ring around the collar" commercials). A wife will be sanctioned by friends and family for keeping a cluttered and dusty home; a husband will not be. Husbands' behaviors are constrained as well. A husband who is content with a relatively low-wage, low-stress occupation may be pressured (by his wife, among others) to provide more for his family. Few wives, however, are pressured into higher-stress, higher-wage occupations by their families. The expectations we face during ongoing interaction often push us to behave as others want us to (Heiss 1981).

Cultural images within marriage also make gendered action possible. Husbands are not free to work long hours in order to climb the career ladder or increase income unless they are superordinate partners in a system in which wives provide them the "leisure" (i.e., freedom from responsibility for self-care or family care) to do so. Some married women may leave jobs they dislike because the position of domestic wife is open to them. A husband and father unable to keep a job has few other options for gaining self-esteem and identity.

Individuals often act in a structurally patterned fashion, without much thought. Routine is taken for granted even when the action re-creates the inequitable social structure. A woman may choose to change her name upon marriage simply because it seems easier. (Some women may not even know they are making a choice, as name change is so routine in their social circle.) Yet by changing her name a woman implicitly supports and re-creates a reflective definition of wifehood. She does gender. Similarly, when a woman assents to her children carrying her husband's surname (even when she herself has retained her own), she is re-creating a patrilineal system by which family identity is traced primarily through the male line. In both these examples a couple's intention may be to create a nuclear family identity and to avoid the awkwardness of hyphenated names for children. Whatever the intention, the structure has constrained the possible choices available to them. Their purposive actions may provide them with both the desired consequences (one family name) *and* the unintended consequence of re-creating a gender structure based on reflective female identity and patrilineal family names.

Let us now turn to a more concrete illustration of my thesis: how gender as a structure at the interactional level, in combination with the existence of gendered work institutions, can create inequality despite the motivations of the actors. To illustrate this hypothesis I will weave a story about a young feminist couple who marry while both are pursuing graduate degrees.[6] Although this story is fictional, I have taken every aspect from real people's lives — my own graduate students' struggles, stories from colleagues and their spouses, my own family members and friends, and my own experiences.

The graduate students in my story marry. The couple retain their own names and explicitly agree to pursue a fully egalitarian relationship. The husband's family immediately question the relationship because the wife will not even embrace their name. And the husband himself cannot help but notice that some of his colleagues have more time to study because their wives are temporarily supporting them rather than pursuing their own careers. Some of his friends' wives even type papers, and most prepare meals regularly.

How are these events the consequences of gender structure? They are structural constraints in that the cultural expectations for behaviors are attached to the sex category itself. Gendered expectations are cultural objects to which others must respond. No husband is expected to change his name, and few are expected

6. This example is clearly race and class specific. Only a white, middle-class woman would face these particular gender structures. I believe that a multilevel theory of gender will help explain any social context, but I chose the one that I know best in order to illustrate my argument.

to regularly prepare meals for the family. In addition, each partner draws comparisons with similarly situated others. The husband compares himself with other young husbands. What are the experiences of the men with whom he socializes? How available are more service-oriented wives? He compares himself with other men in a male-dominated society. The wife compares herself with other young wives. How egalitarian are their husbands? She may, in fact, notice that there seems to be a shortage of males interested in divesting themselves of male privilege. If they are in a social network with some other egalitarian couples, however, the comparisons will in fact enable their choices. The sociological ambivalence will allow them to negotiate a more feminist lifestyle.

The gender stratification crisis in egalitarian couples can usually be traced to the assigning of parental duties. What happens to an avidly feminist middle-class couple motivated to share these duties equally? At the birth of the first child the male is quickly constrained to be a "good provider." He is considered solely responsible for the economic well-being of this fragile new person. No matter how involved a new father becomes in child care he almost never considers less than full-time employment (Gerson 1993). Feminist men share child care duties before and after paid work. In fact, men are expected to work harder and are constrained from leaving less than optimal jobs because of their economic responsibilities. When they do care for their children after work they are praised highly by friends, family members, and wives as wonderful, modern, "involved" fathers. A married professional woman faces a quite different set of reactions at the birth of the first child. Her domestic women friends and perhaps even her own family members may suggest that she is a selfish feminist who puts herself before her own child's welfare. If the child is clingy, friends may suggest that the child doesn't get to see the mother very much (even though the child sees her just as often as she or he sees the wonderful father these friends rave about). If the child is independent they suggest that this trait comes from having to fend for herself or himself too often and too soon. Although the wife provides at least as much care as her husband, he is praised and she is damned. The couple themselves begin to think of him as a terrific father and of her as a reasonable if somewhat selfish mother. His self-esteem is high, and she feels lucky to have such a husband, given the alternatives. The culturally defined cognitive images and the gendered rules are taking their toll.

Then the second child is born. The scarcity of high-quality infant care forces the parents to spend an extra hour daily commuting to two different child-care providers. Both parents feel tired and pressured. The husband never considers working part-time because the "good provider" expectation does not allow it. In fact, he knows how much his advancement has been hindered by his need to leave the office every day at 5:30 sharp to dash to the day-care center before it closes. He understands that he is fast falling behind his male colleagues in more traditional families. At the same time, his wife compares herself with both employed and stay-at-home mothers. She sees the emotional costs of maintaining a two-career family. This young mother does not compare herself with the ambitious men in her husband's office who work ten-hour days. Rather, she compares herself with the other women in the social welfare agency in which she works and with women who do not work for pay at all. Perhaps she finds less satisfaction and fewer material rewards in the workplace than she had hoped for during her graduate training. Like most women, she works in a sex-segregated environment in which she and her colleagues are undervalued and underpaid. Most of her colleagues also struggle to balance family and economic responsibilities. She decides that despite the financial hardship, part-time employment will give her the best of both worlds. She may even be surprised at the personal satisfaction that parenting has provided her, and, unlike her husband, she is not glued to her occupation by the breadwinner expectations. In fact, if she can arrange to work when her husband is home, the savings in day-care costs may result in an only marginal decrease in family income. She feels lucky; she will retain her professional identity and skills while slowing the hectic pace of their lives. Her husband is pleased to have the freedom to commit himself to career mobility. Her purposive action, chosen after much deliberation, will provide the desired consequences.

The powerful effects of both the institutional and the interactional aspects of the gender structure become more apparent as the story continues. The institutional components of the gender structure include a sex-segregated labor force, a wage gap, the lack of available, accessible, excellent infant care, and full-time employment usually defined as forty or more uninterrupted hours per week. Social institutions continue to operate as if workers have domestic wives, disadvantaging men and women who do not. The cultural images or gender rules also are constraining: the breadwinner image only to him, and the domestic wife image only to her.

Thompson's (1991) application of distributive justice theory to family studies explains why a self-consciously feminist woman will not necessarily perceive any inequity as her marriage falls into a traditional pattern. Gender has so structured her perceptions that her reference group is single-sex. She may not "have it all," but compared with other women (historically and in her circle), she has more. Lennon and Rosenfeld (1994) show empirically that only when women have real economic alternatives to marriage do they even begin to define their double burden or limited choices as unfair.

The combination of gendered institutions and cognitive images based on gender rules lead this feminist couple to discover a gendered strategy: part-time employment for the woman. But the unintended consequence of this action will have a profound impact on their marriage. And the unintended consequence of this alternative (from the structurally available options) by many women is to support and re-create gender stratification in both marital and economic institutions. The negotiated order has fallen under the constraints of gender structure. This woman has become an economic dependent, and as a partner in the marital exchange she is at a disadvantage. They may be equals in the exchange of companionship, love, and sexual fulfillment, but he has now become the primary source of economic support. The longer she remains outside the full-time labor force the less capable she will be of supporting herself and her children. The longer she works part-time, the more financially dependent she becomes.

The unintended consequences of "choosing" this path go far beyond the dynamics of the marital relationships of women who are employed part-time. Like domestic wives, these women provide the hidden labor that supports an economic system that continues to operate as if workers are disembodied people with no family responsibilities. The firm where her husband works can expect ambitious employees to work long hours only if there are enough workers with wives who will provide domestic service. And because some women provide hidden labor, those workers who have children but do not have domestic wives will find it hard to compete with men in traditional marriages. Indeed, those who rise to the top, the professional and elite gatekeepers, are usually childless individuals or men with wives at home. Thus, people with caretaking responsibilities are unlikely to reach such levels of power or influence (see Hunt and Hunt 1977).

The issue of part-time employment for women is perhaps the best illustration of the tenacity of our stratified gender structure. And it is no trivial issue. Analysis of current national data (Hayghe and Bianchi 1994) shows that in 1992 only 36.8 percent of married mothers worked full-time, full-year for pay. About an equal number (36.1 percent) work in the labor force part-time or part of the year, and the rest (27.1 percent) depend solely on their husband's economic support. Although the high percentage of employed women has garnered much attention, only a minority of married women work full-time. And many professionally successful women either choose to remain childless or to devote themselves to careers only after their children are gone. Employers continue to assume that the most successful and ambitious workers will have wives or do not need them. And the empirical reality is still that most men do not have major nurturing responsibilities, either for children or for the aged. The presumption that the "best" employee must be willing to work long, inflexible hours has left many families with only bad choices. The irony is that when married couples choose (that is, take the least unattractive option) for the wife to work part-time, they are re-creating gender stratification in their own marriage and in the economic sector. Part-time employment for married women —often the least unattractive of available options—may provide just enough illusion of gender equality to allow the institutional structural inequities to remain entrenched.

Summary

I have argued that gender is a social structure. It organizes our entire world. At the individual level we learn who we are and want to be within a world where boys and girls are treated almost as though they were different kinds of creatures. At the interactional level our expectations for others' behaviors are filtered through a gender lens (Howard et al. 1996). The cultural rules and cognitive images that give shape and substance to our daily lives—especially those rules and images that surround our most intimate relationships—are profoundly attached to our biological sex. As the twentieth century closes, much of the formal, legalized, institutional sex discrimination has been eliminated, at least in Western societies. But the formal institutions to which we must all adapt—our workplaces, in particular—were built on assumptions both of gender difference and sexual inequality. Industrial capitalism could never have been organized as it now exists unless there was an implicit belief that paid workers were not, or should not be, responsible for the weak, the infirm, the aged, or the young.

The gender structure so pervades our lives that we often do not even see it. We fail to recognize that these differential expectations for men and women, for husbands and wives, are how sexual difference is transformed into gender stratification. I have argued that our gender structure at the interactional level is at the core of the male privilege still obvious in marriage and the family and that the structure of our interactional encounters re-creates gender stratification even when the people involved are committed to equality.

But does this theoretical perspective mean that we are doomed forever to re-create gender inequality? In the next three chapters I hope to convince the reader that gender is a social structure that we can get beyond. Gender need not organize our family systems, even if it always has done so.

3

Necessity and the Invention of Mothering

What happens when individuals find themselves in ambiguous situations, when gendered selves are socialized for traditional family life but current interactional contexts shift? How flexible are we? Can men mother even if they have never dressed or bathed a doll? Male mothering isn't common, not now and not in the past. But is it possible?

All three levels of the gender structure push most men and women toward gendered lives and choices. Sometimes, however, this structure is disrupted; the planned courses of family lives are changed by unexpected circumstances (see, e.g., Gerson 1993). In this chapter, I acknowledge the macro-institutional aspects of the gender structure, which organize both family and work so as to support male advantage in the marketplace and female responsibility in the home. I focus on how individuals fare when the parental roles that men are socialized for (in this case, to be breadwinner fathers) are radically altered and men find themselves the sole caretakers of young children. Do gendered selves make "mothering" problematic for men? Or do the interactional expectations of their roles as custodial parents shape their lives more directly?

Although men have been involved at some places and times in the rearing of children—particularly boys old enough to be incorporated in economic labor—we use the phrase "mothering" because the nurturing of children has mostly been women's work.[1] This responsibility for the day-to-day nurturing that we have come to call mothering is, perhaps, the aspect of gender structure most constant across time and cultures.

Although I call mothering women's work, I do not mean to imply that it has not also been women's joy. The word "work" sometimes calls forth negative connotations: hard, unpleasant, performed only as an obligation. I use the word quite differently. Work must get done for a society to exist, yet working—doing what needs to ensure collective and individual survival—can and should be fun, fulfilling, and able to provide meaning for our very existence. Perhaps mothering is the best example of that positive kind of work—work that involves the shaping of human beings can be especially creative and fulfilling. And such work is of course critical to the survival of any society.

Can only women do this work well? Can only women be effective as primary nurturers? The answer is crucial, for no one would want to abolish gender structure at the cost of harming our children. But I do not believe that sexual equality and a post-gendered society would hurt future generations of children. My research suggests that men *can* mother.

Scholars and researchers who work at the individual level of analysis do not agree on this issue. Socialization theorists and feminists who adhere to a revisionist psychoanalytic tradition argue that childhood experiences determine the psychic predisposition to

---

1. Pruett (1987) argues that there may be more married nurturing fathers than we know because they are an "underground" phenomenon. He suggests that because societal expectations teach men that they ought to keep their distance from infants and focus on economic security, men who do otherwise might choose to hide their involvement. Nevertheless, Pruett's interview study is based on a small sample of married fathers referred to him from his own and others' pediatric practices.

mothering (Chodorow 1978; Gilligan 1982). If we change the way we treat our sons and daughters, they argue, we could rear a generation of boys and girls who are equally capable as nurturers. Biosocial theorists, however, use evolutionary, genetic, and hormonal evidence to suggest that women have a biological predisposition to bonding with and caring for infants, although compensatory training is sometimes suggested to overcome these biological impediments to male nurturing (see Rossi 1984 for this argument). But all individual-level theories maintain that the desire to mother (or not) is the result of an internalized gendered identity. The implicit presumption often made by those who study individuals is that this internalized psychological motivation is why women nurture their children so intensively and men do not.

Interactional Bases of Mothering

As I argued in the last chapter, rules that are part of the gender structure at the interactional level can be conceptualized as folklore or as cognitive images that must be attended to when considering one's own actions. We face such images in every interpersonal relationship. There is rarely any sociological ambivalence in the cognitive images of parenthood, even today. Mothers, employed or not, are still expected to nurture their children emotionally and physically. Fathers are still expected to earn a family wage, even when that is not possible. Fathers are also expected to help mothers with nurturing, but they are not judged incompetent if they do not help very much as long as they continue to earn a good living.

Not all mothers or fathers turn this folk story into reality, but all are aware of the normatively accepted cognitive images. And the research on dual-earner couples shows that these images are indeed powerful organizers of many lives. Even when both parents work for pay the children and the home remain primarily the wife's responsibility (Brines 1994; Berardo, Shehan, and Leslie 1987; Berk

1985; Coverman 1983). Hochschild (1989) estimates that employed wives spend the equivalent of a month a year doing the "second shift" at home, thus adding appreciably to their work time. Such inequity exists only because it is invisible, hidden by the strong cultural beliefs about the natural bases of nurturance and mothering. Fathers are not usually expected to nurture their children intensively, but because children demand such nurturing, the cognitive images blur somewhat for single fathers. The status of single parent overrides sex category for the expectations of and demands made on single fathers not only by their children but also by friends, family members, and the educational system. The gender theory that I propose predicts that the consequences of gender structure at the interactional level, the situational demands, and the clearly expressed need of young children to be nurtured will create behaviors in men that are usually called "mothering." My hypothesis is that the consequences of gender structure at the interactional level are more powerful predictors of gendered parenting than are gendered selves.

To test these ideas I compared the parental behaviors and household strategies of single fathers with those of single mothers, dual-paycheck couples, and traditional mother-at-home families. If individual-level factors like socialization or biology are the keys to parental behavior, single fathers would have neither the motivation nor the skills to provide appropriate primary care for children; their care would not be equivalent to that provided by mothers. If, however, interactional factors are more influential, the father can take on the primary caretaker role and fulfill expectations for adequate care made by extended family, schools, and neighbors and the children themselves. He will produce mothering that is very similar to that provided by a woman in the same situation.

My own study on single fathers was designed to test the relative power of individual-level versus interactional explanations for empirically observable sex differences in parenting styles (Risman 1987). But before presenting the findings of that study I will mention what we know about single fathers from other sources.

Review of the Literature on Single Fathers

There has been much debate over the important question of how children who live in single-parent households thrive versus those who live with both parents. That is not my concern here. Instead, I focus on how single fathers and single mothers are similar and different, and why.

Descriptive findings about single fathers are remarkably consistent across studies (Chang and Deinard 1982; Gasser and Taylor 1976; George and Wilding 1972; Greenberg 1979; Hanson 1981; Mendes 1979; Orthner, Brown, and Ferguson 1976; Risman 1986; Rosenthal and Keshet 1981). Homemaking does not appear to be a problem for single fathers—few recruit female kin or paid help to perform the "female" tasks of housekeeping. And although American single fathers do report some problems, such as worrying because their daughters lack a female role model, most respondents generally feel satisfied with their perceived competence as single parents and single adults.

Unfortunately, much of the research on American men who are single fathers does not compare them with other men or with single mothers. It simply describes small samples of predominantly white, middle-class fathers (Ambert 1982; Defrain and Eirick 1981; Gasser and Taylor 1976; Greenberg 1979; Hanson 1981; Mendes 1979; Orthner, Brown, and Ferguson 1976; Risman 1986; Rosenthal and Keshet 1981; Santrock and Warshak 1979). The fathers in these samples usually are identified from such sources as parent organizations, media advertisements, and referrals, and they frequently have similar incomes and reasons for custody.

It is particularly problematic that American research has been based on such homogeneous samples, because English and Australian studies, which include more economically deprived families, suggest that financial status is a key factor in men's performance and satisfaction as single fathers (e.g., Ferri 1973; Hipgrave 1982; Murch 1973). In one large sample (George and Wilding 1972), fathers who reported financial problems also felt less competent as parents. Similarly, researchers whose samples include many financially deprived families (Katz 1979; O'Brien 1982) tend to report more serious problems in both father-child relationships and father's role satisfaction.

There is a small body of research that does explicitly compare single fathers and single mothers concerning their parental behaviors and their children's development (Ambert 1982; Defrain and Eirick 1981; Downey and Powell 1993; Grief 1985; Hanson 1986; Luepnitz 1986; Pett and Vaughan-Cole 1986; Rosen 1979; Santrock and Warshak 1979; Warshak 1986; Schnayer and Orr 1989). These studies can be used to address the relative causal importance of individualist and interactional factors on parenting behaviors. Although the studies vary greatly in scope and methodological strength, they all suggest that variables other than parental sex greatly affect parent-child relationships in single-parent homes.[2]

2. There is some debate on whether there is interaction between parent's and child's sex; that is, whether boys do better living with their fathers and girls with their mothers. Santrock, Warshak, and Elliot (1982) found that children living with same-sex parents were more socially competent, less angry, less demanding, and warmer than those living with opposite-sex custodial parents, but Rosen's research (1979) did not replicate these findings. Downey and Powell (1993) designed a study with a random sample of American teenagers and their parents and report absolutely no data to support the notion that children do better with same-sex parents. My own reading of this research is that there is no indication that children, as a rule, do better with one parent or another simply on the basis of whether the child is the same or the opposite sex.

The results are remarkably consistent: there are few differences in either parental satisfaction or child's development based on the sex of the parent. The results are similar whether the findings are based on small samples with an intensive study of each child's development (Santrock and Warshak 1979; Rosen 1979) or on somewhat larger studies using primarily quantitative measures of parents' attitudes and children's development (Luepnitz 1986).

One study reports an important and significant difference between children living with single mothers and with single fathers. Hanson (1986) found that children in single-father homes were slightly less physically healthy than those living with their mothers. The reverse was true for the parents: the fathers were healthier than the mothers. This finding, which seems to contradict most of the rest of the evidence, is based on a nonrepresentative sample of forty-two custodial parents recruited by the author. Still, it is the only study I know of that deals with health issues, and it indicates a need for further study on this topic.

Downey and Powell (1993) have provided a methodologically sophisticated study based on a nationally representative sample. Unfortunately, their question is even narrower than mine: Do children do better living with same-sex or opposite-sex parents after divorce? Still, I have found in their tables important information that sheds light on the more general question about gender differences in single parenting. Downey and Powell collected data from parents and their eighth-grade children. They found that when children living with single mothers and single fathers are compared with one another, the eighth-graders living with their *fathers* appeared to be doing better on social-psychological and educational standardized tests. But what was really happening was that children living with more well-to-do parents were scoring better on these tests, and most of the fathers were doing better economically than were the mothers. Given the well-documented gender gap in wages

(Reskin and Padavic 1994) it should not be surprising that fathers earn higher salaries, on average, than do mothers. Once the effect of income was controlled statistically, however, the fathers' advantage disappeared. There are, instead, a few developmental advantages for children living with their mothers. Still, the major finding from this research is that there are few differences between single fathers and mothers as parents at least as measured by their children's development. (This does not differ whether the parent and child are the same or the opposite sex.)

In sum, the comparative research offers strong support for the importance of the interactional context in explaining gender-typed behavior. Nearly all the research published by others indicates that when fathers cannot depend on wives for child care, those fathers develop parenting behaviors similar to those of women. My own research was designed to further substantiate this hypothesis.

Can Men "Mother"?

In order to study this question I had to locate single fathers. This is not easy now, and it was even harder in the early 1980s. I advertised in national single-parent magazines and solicited referrals from social service agencies in Seattle and Boston. Volunteers were recruited through radio talk shows and public service announcements across the country. Word-of-mouth referrals were also used. This nonrandom, volunteer sample has limited generalizability. There were, however, no sampling frames from which to draw a random sample of single fathers. And I wanted a very particular kind of single father. I did not want to study only a self-selected group of "feminine" men who for some reason intensely desired to nurture children. I wanted to study men whose wives had died or had deserted the family—that is, men who were "reluctant" single fathers (cf. Gerson 1985) who ended up as nurturers through no choice of their own. Such a group is the perfect naturally occurring field in which to test the relative strength of internalized self and interactional determinants for gender-typed behavior.[3] (For technical information about sample selection and demographics, or any technical aspect of the analyses, see Risman 1987.)

Reluctant Single Fathers and Comparison Groups

Between 1981 and 1983, I distributed questionnaires to 281 single fathers. The response rate was 54 percent (141 surveys completed). To meet eligibility requirements for this research the father had to have a child under thirteen years of age who was a full-time resident in the home, and the father's custody had to be the result of widowhood, desertion, or the ex-wife's disinterest in shared responsibility. These criteria ensured that the single fathers lived alone with young children through circumstances beyond their control. Only 55 of the 141 volunteer respondents met all the criteria for participation in the analyses.[4]

The single mothers, the dual-paycheck parents, and the traditional parents were identified from the same referral sources as the single fathers whenever possible. Additional single mothers and married parents were recruited at Seattle-area day-care centers, day camps, public school open houses, sports classes at YMCAs, and boys' and girls' clubs. During eighteen months of data collection,

3. Even so, my sample is not without possible problems. Widowers are the only pure case of male primary caretakers who could not have been selected for their nurturing capabilities. And even widowed men who do not or cannot respond to the demands of single parenthood probably remarry quickly. Deserted fathers are also somewhat problematic because a woman who trusts her husband's ability to be the primary parent may be more likely to desert her children. Nevertheless, short of designing an ethically impossible experiment, this is the best sample that I could envision.

4. For articles based on research using the entire sample of 141 volunteers see Risman 1986 or 1988.

126 questionnaires were distributed to single mothers and 73 were completed, for a response rate of 58 percent. Married couples received 350 questionnaires; 155 husbands and wives returned their surveys in separate envelopes, yielding a return rate of 44 percent. The response rate for married respondents was lower than for single parents because some spouses were unwilling to return questionnaires for a study for which only one partner had volunteered. Neither spouse was considered a respondent if only one returned the survey.

Each of the families headed by a single father was matched to one family in each other category (single mother, married two-paycheck, married traditional) by the age of the youngest child. Nearly all respondents were white. There were no statistically significant differences in the sex composition of the sibling groups. The economic status of these respondents varied tremendously. Families headed by two parents were more affluent than those headed by single parents, even if only one parent in the couple was in the labor force. Although the single mothers were by far the poorest of the respondents, they earned considerably more than single mothers nationally; almost half reported annual incomes between $20,000 and $30,000. The single fathers reported higher incomes than the single mothers, but their incomes were lower than those of the married men respondents. Most of the married couples in the sample were better off financially than the average American family (U.S. Department of Commerce 1980), with more than 75 percent reporting annual family incomes above $30,000. (Note that these income figures are from the early 1980s. In 1996 that $30,000 was the equivalent of about $44,000 [U.S. Bureau of the Census 1995].)

There were significant differences in occupational status by gender. The men were more likely than the employed women to work in professional and blue-collar jobs, the women more likely than the men to work in clerical and sales positions. These differences explain some of the economic disparities between the single mothers and single fathers in the sample.

Measures

All the measures I used in these analyses were constructed from a twenty-page questionnaire on the relationship between the parent and his or her child. If the parent had two or more children under thirteen the questionnaire asked him or her to think about the youngest child. The respondent's sex represents the individualist factor, based on the assumption that if biological predispositions or sex-based socialization does indeed lead to internalized masculine and feminine personalities, then parental strategies should differ simply by respondent's sex, whatever adult social role is adopted. Although I have no measure of the parents' childhood socialization, I am using the simple—and I hope reasonable—assumption that these parents were raised in an era when being a boy or a girl determined a great deal of one's sex-role socialization. Sex category is an ideal measure for whatever biological imperatives might exist to shape parenting behaviors.

A weakness in this scheme is clearly that being male or female influences both how one is raised and the kinds of expectations and cultural cues one faces as an adult. Therefore, any differences that we find in the parenting styles of single mothers and fathers might be as much the result of their internalized gendered selves as the differing expectations because of their sex. Fortunately, a *lack* of sex differences in parenting styles can be clearly attributed only to the expectations attached to being a primary caretaker. Given that my hypothesis is that family role factors will overcome individualist factors, this measurement weakness actually makes it harder for me to be right. In a statistical sense, the design is biased against my hypothesis, a very conservative scientific strategy.

The interactional context was operationalized by parental role. The first variable was whether the parent is primarily responsible for child care, with all single parents and homemakers considered primarily responsible. The second variable contrasts married parents, both of whom are employed full-time, with the other respondents (home workers, dual-worker parents, and single parents). These two-worker families are referred to as role-sharers because both partners perform the breadwinner role, not because of any a priori presumption that they have shared household labor equally. When both variables are included in the analyses, traditional male breadwinners married to full-time female homemakers are used as a comparison group (and, in statistically analytic terms, the omitted group).

The parental role variables (primary caretaker, role-sharer, and breadwinner) are used to try to capture the salience of the interactionist-level of gender structure, the power of immediate expectations and social context. I again use simple reasoning: single parents, male or female, and married homemakers are primarily responsible for the intensive day-to-day work of rearing their children. Single parents can depend on no one else, and married homemakers are, at least temporarily, specializing in child care as full-time work. Men married to homemakers are specializing in breadwinning, and men and women married to other full-time workers are both juggling two worlds.

The measures for self-definition are based on Bem's (1974) Sex Role Inventory (BSRI) and are designed to measure each parent's psychological masculinity and femininity. BSRI, one of the standard measures in psychology, assesses the respondents' perceptions of their own personalities. It includes sixty semantic differential items on which subjects rate themselves. Each respondent judges how much (from "always" to "not at all") they can be described by adjectives provided on a long list, including "warm," "aggressive," "supportive," and "dominant." Scores are based on the arithmetic mean of responses to the twenty items designed to measure femininity and the twenty items designed to measure masculinity.[5]

BSRI measures are typically assumed to be individualist measures of personality characteristics—to pick up some internalized sense of self as masculine or feminine or both.[6] My interactionist hypothesis, however, suggests that selves are created, sustained, and changed by ongoing, face-to-face interaction. Therefore, measures of self-identity cannot be assumed to be individualist personality measures.

I chose three aspects of mothering to study: making a house into a home, parent-child intimacy, and overt affection. All of my information was based on what the respondents reported on the survey. Even recent research (Brines 1994; Berardo, Shehan, and Leslie 1987; Berk 1985; Coverman 1983; Hochschild 1989) finds that married men are particularly resistant to keeping house, and it is important to see whether this is also true of single fathers who

5. There has been considerable controversy (Strahan 1975; Orlofsky, Aslin, and Ginsburg 1977; Bem 1977) over how masculinity and femininity scores ought to be used to categorize persons as highly masculine, highly feminine, undifferentiated (i.e., low on both scores), and androgynous (i.e., high on both scores). The controversy is not pertinent here because classification of subjects into types would have resulted in loss of information. I am interested in the subjects' perceptions of themselves as both masculine and feminine independently.

6. Despite having created the Bem Sex Role Inventory, Bem (1993) has repudiated the notion that we should even ascribe such personality descriptions as "sensitive" and "dominant" to femininity or masculinity. Such a use of language simply supports an inaccurate understanding of gender, and of men and women. I agree. In the future we should not code personality traits as masculine or feminine. Nevertheless, much research in the past—mine included—has continued to use the language while testing the validity of the individualist ideas.

have no one to else to depend on to turn their houses into homes. Homemaking was measured on a seven-item scale tapping reported personal responsibility for such tasks as cooking, cleaning, and food shopping. The other aspects of mothering that I studied—parent-child intimacy and affection—are much more focused on the tenor and ambience of the relationships so crucial to "good-enough" mothering (Chodorow 1978). Each of these variables was created by adding answers to several questions. All scales are based on the parents' reports of their own and their child's behavior, and results may of course be contaminated by biases in reporting. The self-disclosure scale taps relationship intimacy and includes ten items on how often, in the parents' estimation, a child shares his or her positive and negative emotions. The level of affection that parents report displaying for their child was measured on a three-item additive scale, including a report of the quality of time spent with the child, how often the child was hugged or cuddled, and how often the parent showed physical affection toward the child. See table 3.1 for the exact questions used to measure these concepts.

Research Design

With my research I address aspects of parenting that are typically done differently by men and women: homemaking, showing affection, and developing intimacy with children (fig. 3.1). These are my dependent variables. I have used the questions in table 3.1 to try to capture how these parents see their lives.

The placement of "masculinity" and "femininity" in the middle of figure 3.1 indicates my belief that *both* individualist and interactional factors help to shape how people see themselves as masculine or feminine and that this self-image in turn affects parenting styles. The arrow from these psychological measures to the dependent variables shows that I expect the respondents' definitions of themselves will help explain how they parent.

Table 3.1. Measurement of Parenting Variables

Housework

Who in your family is responsible for the following tasks?

- cooking evening meal
- cleaning the house
- shopping for groceries
- shopping for children's clothing
- laundry
- making breakfast
- making lunch

Intimacy

How likely is your child to share and express the following feelings with you when they occur?

- sadness
- loneliness
- anger
- worry
- anger at you
- happiness
- excitement
- pride
- intelligence
- bravery

Overt Affection

- During the times you focus particular attention on this child alone, how would you characterize the time you spend together?
- How often do you hug or cuddle this child?
- How often do you show physical affection to this child (i.e., cuddling or wrestling)?

Figure 3.1. Empirical Design to Test Alternative
Hypotheses for Gendered Parenting

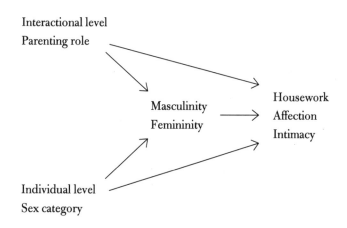

My major hypothesis is that many of the sex differences we see
in homemaking, parent-child intimacy, and parental affection are
better explained by parental role (or interactional factors) than by
parent's sex (an individualist factor). At this point I will switch from
the theoretical language of individualist and interactional levels of
the gender structure to the language of variables as I discuss my
analyses in terms of variables measured.

Findings

Parental role and respondent's sex influenced reports of parent-
child affection almost equally. Women and role-sharers were the
most affectionate. The parental role was an important predictor of
reported parent-child affection, but in an unexpected way. Men
and women who shared responsibility for child care reported being
more physically affectionate with their children than did men and

Table 3.2. Means and Standard Deviations of Endogenous Variables
Used in Regression Equations

	Mean	Standard deviation	Number
Masculinity	6.6	.92	296
Femininity	6.5	.72	307
Housework	2.2	.93	278
Intimacy	7.7	1.15	328
Affect	5.3	.93	319

Note: The number of cases varies because of missing data. No pattern
for missing data was detected. Pairwise deletion of missing data was
used in scale construction.

women who were either primary caretakers or traditional fathers.
Sex itself, however, also remained a powerful predictor of parents'
reports of physical expressions of affection, with women reporting
being more affectionate than men. Perhaps, as Pleck and Sawyer
(1974) suggest, gendered socialization is especially effective in in-
stilling inexpressiveness in men. Or perhaps respondents reported
what they perceived to be socially desirable behavior. Overall, these
analyses suggest the importance (but not exclusivity) of the interactional context for explaining the level of reported parental affection. Both interactional context and gendered selves clearly mattered here. Tables 3.2, 3.3, and 3.4 display the data and equations
that form the bases of these analyses. An understanding of regression analysis is not necessary to follow my argument, but the data
are presented for the interested reader.

These findings show that reported responsibility for housework
is better explained by parental role than by sex. Primary parents,
whether men or women (housewives or single parents), reported
doing much more housework than other parents. Further analy-

Table 3.3. Zero-Order Correlations for Variables Used in Regression Equations

	Sex	Share	Primary	Intimacy	Physical affection	Housework	Femininity	Masculinity
Sex		.0	.33***	.20***	.30***	.57***	.29***	-.25***
Share			-.71***	.10	.10	-.10	-.14	-.02
Primary				.011	.09	.55***	.28***	-.03
Intimacy					.43***	.17**	.35***	.08
Physical affection						.27***	.21***	.04
Housework							.26***	-.15**
Femininity								.47***

Note: Primary and Share are dummy variables with yes coded as 1 and male coded as 0. Sex is a dummy variable with female coded as 1 and male coded as 0.

*p ≤ .05; **p ≤ .01; ***p ≤ .001.

Table 3.4. Reduced and Structural Equations for Housework, Intimacy, and Affection

Dependent Variables	Sex	Primary	Share	Role Priority	Femininity	Masculinity	R2
(1A) Housework	—	—	—				.56***
	(.55)***	(1.23)***	(.80)***				
(1B) Housework	—	—	—	-.04	.06	-.07	.56***
	(.50)***	(1.23)***	(.81)***	(-.02)	(.07)	(-.06)	
(2A) Affection	—	—	—				.11***
	(.47)***	(.20)	(.38)*				
(2B) Affection	—	—	—	.04	.12	.04	.12***
	(.43)***	(.13)	(.37)	(.02)	(.16)	(.04)	
(3A) Intimacy	—	—	—				.03**
	(.28)*	(.35)	(.25)				
(3B) Intimacy	—	—	—	.12*	.38	-.07	.13***
	(.04)	(.16)	(.23)	(.08)	(.55)***	(-.08)	

Note: Both standardized and metric regression coefficients are reported for continuous variables, with metric coefficients in parentheses. Metric coefficients are reported only for dichotomous dummy variables. Role priority was included in equation 3B for the study published elsewhere.

*p ≤ .05; **p ≤ .01; ***p ≤ .001.

Table 3.5. Reduced and Structural Equations for Housework by Sex

	Predictor Variables			
	Men		Women	
	Share	Primary	Share	Primary
Housework	—	—	—	
	(.55)**	(1.28)**	(−.17)**	
	R^2=.46**		R^2=.10*	a

Note: Metric coefficients are reported only because they are dichotomous dummy variables.

a All women—single mothers and housewives—who do not share roles are primary caretakers; therefore, primary drops out of the equation because there is no variation in this cell.

*$p \leq .01$; **$p \leq .001$.

sis found, however, that parental role, particularly for dual-worker couples, affected men and women differently. (In statistical terms, there was an interaction between role and sex.) Therefore, we must look at men and women separately to understand exactly what is going on (see table 3.5). Employed women reported doing some-what less housework than homemakers do. Men married to these employed women report doing significantly more housework than do men married to homemakers. For men, more than half of all the variation in reported responsibility for housework can be attributed to parental role. Simply knowing whether a father is married to a homemaker, has an employed wife, or is single can help to predict the extent of his homemaking activities. Therefore, the hypothesis that much of the variation in housework often attributed to sex can be better explained by situational exigencies is strongly supported when single fathers' lives are examined.

Table 3.6. Mean Femininity and Masculinity Scores

	Femininity	Masculinity
Traditional father	6.31	6.79
Dual-paycheck father	6.34	6.96
Single father	6.54	6.86
Single mother	6.95	6.47
Dual-paycheck mother	6.61	6.23
Traditional mother	6.98	6.43

Note: Range = 1 to 9; 1 = low.

Respondents' sex and parenting role appeared to be equally strong predictors of reported parent-child intimacy. But this analysis was complicated when the respondents' perceptions of their own masculinity and femininity were added to the analysis: the effect of the respondent's sex almost disappeared, but the effect of sharing roles was only slightly weakened. Thus far I have discussed how either parental role or respondent's sex directly affected the dependent variables because there were no statistically significant indirect findings to report. But here the analysis gets slightly more complex. The respondents' sex affected how "feminine" they thought themselves to be. That is, as expected, women described themselves as more feminine than men did. But, more interesting, single fathers described themselves as more feminine than did other men (see table 3.6).

When parental role, respondent's sex, and definition of self were considered simultaneously, femininity was by far the strongest predictor of reported parent-child intimacy. Those men and women who described themselves as having more feminine personality traits reported more intimate relationships with their children (table 3.7). I could quadruple the predictive quality of the analyses (from

Table 3.7. Structural Equations for Femininity and Masculinity

Dependent Variables	Predictor Variables			
	Sex	Primary	Shares	R^2
Femininity	—	—	—	.11**
	(.31)**	(.33)*	(.01)	
Masculinity	—	—	—	.06**
	(−.50)**	(.26)	(.08)	

Note: Metric coefficients are reported only for dichotomous dummy variables.

**$p \leq .01$.

3 to 13 percent) when self-described femininity was included. The respondent's sense of self as measured by the femininity score had an independent effect on reported parent-child intimacy. This was true for men as well as for women. The more a parent described himself or herself with adjectives typically used to measure femininity, the more likely he or she was to report intimacy with children. And single fathers described themselves with more such stereotypically feminine adjectives than did other men.

The finding that parents' femininity scores had an independent effect on reported parent-child intimacy led me to explore the factors that affected how parents see themselves. Individualist theorists presume that socialization creates stable feminine and masculine personality traits, and interactional theory has long suggested that selves are constantly constructed and sustained by the situational experiences in everyday life (Blumstein 1991; Rosenberg 1981; Strauss 1969). Parental role was as good a predictor of self-reported femininity as respondent's sex. In fact, being a primary caretaker (male or female) had a somewhat larger effect than being a woman for predicting self-reported femininity. This is an important finding for the theoretical understanding of gender. Theorists often assume that women are more nurturing than men because they internalized feminine personality traits during socialization. The results suggest that it is just as plausible that at least some women and men display feminine traits because the roles they play demand such characteristics. Social roles—even if not chosen—influence self-perceived femininity. The findings about femininity provide strong support for the flexibility of gendered selves. But the findings on masculinity do not; socialization seems particularly sticky when it comes to masculinity. (For the data on which this discussion has been based, see table 3.7.)

In sum, my study provides empirical support for the importance of the interactional context in determining parenting behavior. The research suggests that parental role is a strong predictor of reported responsibility for housework and reported parent-child affection. Married parents who share the responsibility for child care reported more intimate relationships with their children than did other respondents. Parental role was the only variable directly related to reports of parent-child intimacy. Parental role was as good a predictor of self-reported feminine personality characteristics as biological sex.

My study also shows, however, the concurrent importance of individualist factors for parenting behavior. Sex remained a significant predictor of reported parental physical expressions of affection and had an important but indirect effect on reported parent-child intimacy. In addition, the respondent's sex was a powerful predictor of self-reported masculinity.

Even Better Evidence for the Viability of Male Mothers

When I conducted my research on single fathers I had to depend on a nonrandom sample [7] and therefore could not generalize concerning the results of the surveys. Now, however, there is a nationally representative data set that includes enough single fathers and enough data on the parent-child dyad to study these questions with a more representative sample.

In 1987–88 a National Survey of Families and Households was completed at the University of Wisconsin (Sweet, Bumpass, and Call 1988). A data set was produced from this random survey, which had more than 13,000 respondents, 5,666 of whom reported a child or stepchild under age nineteen living in the household. Twelve and a half percent of the households with children were headed by single mothers, and 1.7 percent were headed by single fathers. These data make it possible to see whether the results based on the volunteer and nonrepresentative samples discussed in this chapter apply to parents selected randomly for a nationally representative study.

Thompson, McLanahan, and Curtin (1992) published research based on this sample that directly supports my argument. Their question was somewhat broader: Why do children in single-parent homes appear disadvantaged as compared with those who live with both parents? A major strategy for finding an answer was to compare single fathers and single mothers with parents in nearly every conceivable family type. In an article based on research about families with children aged five to eighteen, Thompson et al. found that single fathers and single mothers have quite similar parenting styles

7. My requirement that the single fathers in my research be "reluctant" (e.g., widowed or deserted) would have made a random sample prohibitively expensive in any case.

— styles that differ somewhat from those of married parents. Single parents exert weaker controls and make fewer demands on their children than do married parents. In the past, single mothers were assumed to portray this weaker control style because their female socialization had left them unable to be tough (an individual-level gender socialization explanation). The Thompson et al. research shows convincingly that the differences in parenting between single and married parents can be better explained by the contextual interaction factor: the lack of a live-in partner. Single fathers portray this pattern, too.

The interactional effects of family context can also be seen in the Thompson, McLanahan, and Curtin analyses of how many activities fathers and mothers do with their children. Among married parents, the mothers eat with their children more often, do more home activities, take more outings, and organize more youth activities than do fathers. When the responses of single fathers and single mothers are compared, however, they are much more alike than different. At the conclusion of their article, Thompson et al. state that "these results are consistent with Risman's (1987) hypothesis that the micro-structural conditions of parenthood outweigh traditional gender roles in determining parental behavior" (376).

In an even more recent study, Hall, Walker, and Acock (1995) also used this nationally representative sample to compare mothers and fathers as single parents. Like me, they were testing the power of structural variables at the micro level of interaction, such as parental role versus gender socialization as predictors of parent-child relationships and time spent on household work. They report that once demographic and economic variables are statistically controlled, mothers and father do not differ in the number of meals eaten together or in time spent with children in other activities. Some differences remain, however, with fathers spending more leisure time and mothers spending more time in private talks with children. Overall, single mothers did spend more time per week on household labor, but single fathers spent an average of thirty-four hours per week in household labor. They conclude—as do I—that single mothers and fathers are more similar than men and women in two-parent families and that "mothers and fathers in one-parent households do not differ greatly in their interactions with children" (691).

Data better than my own, then, support the importance of the interactional context in how gender structure affects family relationships. When findings from the methodologically weak studies discussed in the beginning of the chapter, my own study based on a strong design but weak sample, and the large and methodologically sophisticated studies using a random sample are all consistent, we can feel confident about the strength of support for the hypothesis.

Conclusion

I am indeed confident, then, that men can mother and that children are not necessarily better nurtured by women than by men. Even men who did not choose to be single fathers were able to invent mothering that works. Some long-term effects of gender socialization do remain, particularly for masculinity, yet I believe that these findings suggest that we can go beyond organizing our world around gender without hurting our children.

Perhaps a better question is, Why don't more men mother? How is it that the vast majority of men leave the intensive day-to-day childrearing and shaping of future generations to women? Even today women provide most of their children's daily care. In a recent study of 138 men Gerson (1993) found only twelve fathers whose involvement with their children matched that of their wives. How can society condone such inequity? The research presented here indicates that we cannot explain men's absence from child care by their lack of capacity to develop the needed skills. And I find it hard to believe that such a nearly universal absence is wholly attributable to preference, because mothering is very rewarding and fulfilling work (McMahon 1995). My answer is that the gender structure has so organized our daily interactions that the consequence of sex-based social responsibilities—gender stratification—is deeply hidden by contemporary folklore about families.

4

Women's Hard Choices

Mothering in the Twentieth Century

Just as men have rarely focused on providing day-to-day, intensive attention to their children, women have nearly always devoted time and attention to mothering. But it was not until the Industrial Revolution that mothering was defined as a full-time job. Previously, women had mothered children in addition to producing goods and services for themselves, their family, and their society. The very notion of motherhood as an occupation is a radical modern invention. Yet this notion has seeped deeply into our consciousness.

Today, many women define motherhood as a career. Nearly one of three married mothers work exclusively in the home, and another third work for pay only part of the time, fitting paid work around their full-time mothering job (Hayghe and Bianchi 1994). Still, of course, that means that two-thirds of married mothers and the majority of single mothers do juggle paid and family work. Few women have any choices: the husband's wages are sometimes too low for families to survive, and other times they are too low for families to achieve the American dream of home ownership. And increasingly, women and children simply have no husbands or fathers willing and able to contribute at all. Yet many women and men still cling to a cultural belief system which suggests that the best option for children is their own mother's full-time attention, and these parents worry about the effect on children if mothers "evacuate" the home to work for money (Coleman 1990). Consider how gendered a notion this is: Have you ever heard anyone worry about the negative effect a father's merely being employed will have on his children?

But there still are a few women who have some choice about how to juggle their paid and family work. Only 36.8 percent of married mothers are employed full-time outside their homes (Hayghe and Bianchi 1994). It may be that some of the married mothers who do not work for pay full-time would prefer to do so if jobs and day care were available. But at least some married mothers choose not to work for pay if they can help it. Empirical research that helps to explain the decisions made by those women who have choices can lead us to understand how gendered families come into existence and perhaps how we can change them.

In this chapter I present longitudinal research that my colleagues and I designed to explain how women who are privileged enough to have a choice about juggling family and work responsibilities make their decisions (Risman, Atkinson, and Blackwelder 1994, 1998).[1] We analyzed data from a group of married women who were first studied as high school students in the mid-1960s and were followed for thirteen years (Otto, Call, and Spenner 1981). We can see how well their childhood socialization and adolescent plans predict their choices. And we can see what other variables—their husbands' income level and their own success on the job, for example—are important in explaining the time devoted to paid and family work.

I must emphasize, however, that few women have such a choice about paid employment. Single women have no choice. Women married to men whose wages cannot lift the family beyond poverty

1. This research was funded by grants from the National Science Foundation (SES #91-23002) and the College of Humanities and Social Sciences at North Carolina State University to Maxine Atkinson and me. For complete technical information about this research see Risman, Atkinson, and Blackwelder 1994, 1998.

have no choice. And no one ever has a choice entirely of her own making. No single woman has the choice of living in a society that supports nurturing her own large family while she holds down a socially valuable but low-wage occupation. For example, a single mother who would like to work in hospice care can hardly make that choice if the day-care costs for her own three young children exceed her paycheck. Nor can a lawyer choose to take the fast track to partnership in a prestigious law firm and expect to see much of her toddler. Yet the fact that only slightly more than one-third of married women work full-time outside their homes suggests that individual women are juggling their responsibilities in different ways. Some of those who are not employed full-time surely would like to be—if jobs existed for them, at wages that covered easily accessible high quality child care. But some women prefer to remain outside the full-time paid labor force if they can. They see an incompatibility between the workplace and mothering, and they choose to minimize paid labor rather than to maximize household income. As a sociologist, I want to know how women are affected by social forces and how they shape their own lives given the constraints that our society imposes upon them.

In *Hard Choices,* Gerson (1985) offers a way to think about women's lives that has influenced my work tremendously. She suggests that we can classify women into two groups according to their childhood goals and expectations: those whose goals were primarily to be wives and mothers (domestic goals) and those who expect to have careers whether or not they expect to have children (work-committed goals). We can then track these women to see whether their lives follow the paths they had planned. When they do not we can try to identify the experiences in adulthood that altered those plans.

Gerson studied a small sample of California working-class and middle-class women born during the 1950s. She found that those who remembered having traditional domestic goals as teenagers were just as likely to be employed full-time in their thirties as they were to have become domestically oriented wives. Similarly, women who remembered intending to stay in the work force whatever family roles they adopted were just as likely to be full-time homemakers as they were to be employed. Therefore, their childhood socialization and adolescent goals were not good predictors of life choices. Much better predictors were the stability of marriage, husband's wages, the existence of career opportunities, and community support for domesticity. In the language that I have proposed, Gerson's data show that the interactional factors experienced in adulthood are much better predictors of women's lives than are internalized gendered selves.

Unfortunately, Gerson's exploratory study alone is not sufficient support for a theoretical explanation of gendered behavior. Her data are based on intensive interviews to elicit the women's life histories. This methodology is perfect for probing deep emotional issues and understanding the complexity of individual lives and is essential for theory building. But it also has drawbacks. The major problem is that sometimes memory fails or, even worse, is distorted or at least reinterpreted in light of more recent events. The women in Gerson's sample remembered how they felt at eighteen, but Gerson did not interview them until they were adults.

My colleagues and I built a replication of Gerson's research into a larger study to see whether we could identify the social forces that would push women toward full-time domesticity or toward labor-force participation (Risman, Atkinson, and Blackwelder 1994, 1996). Our study has the advantage of a longitudinal design; the women filled out surveys when they were juniors and seniors in high school and then again thirteen years later. We built on Gerson's work to further test the relative strength of internalized selves versus interactional factors as explanations for the construction of gendered families. The information provided here will allow the reader to follow the logic and findings of the study but will not replicate earlier technical papers.

The Sample

Although we have information collected over a thirteen-year period, we did not collect it ourselves but instead reanalyzed data from the Career Development Study (CDS) originally collected by Otto, Call, and Spenner (1981). In 1965 and 1966 a team of researchers gathered data from 6,729 high school juniors and seniors from Washington state. The schools were selected to represent a range of economic communities. In 1979 nearly all of these respondents (98.1 percent) were relocated, and 86.9 percent of them (2,877 men and 2,972 women) completed telephone interviews. The now-adult respondents were asked to provide information about their educational achievements, family life, military history, and work experiences. They were asked to recall the month and year that events happened. The respondents were also asked to respond to a mailed questionnaire, which was returned by 73 percent of the original respondents. This is not a nationally representative sample; the respondents came from families that were slightly better off than the norm and that had slightly higher incomes than the average American. Only 2 percent of the original sample was nonwhite, compared with 4 percent of the population in Washington state and 12 percent in the nation at the time. Our study focused on the 1,711 women who were married at the time the final data were collected.

Measures

Gendered selves. Attitudes that coalesced during childhood and adolescence were measured in the adolescent gender-role attitude scale with four questions asked in 1965–66 about the appropriate role for women in society. Respondents indicated their level of agreement with the following statements on a 5-point scale:

1. The abilities of women too often go unrecognized.
2. Women should be allowed to compete on equal terms with men in the occupational world.
3. There would probably be fewer problems in the world if women had as much say-so in running things as men.
4. It is natural for women to have occupational positions which are inferior to those of men.

Higher values are indicative of more traditional values. The mean response was 1.2. Table 4.1 shows the means, standard deviations, and correlations between variables used in the analyses presented in this chapter.

The second measure of socialization concerns the women's hopes and plans for themselves as they finished high school. This measure is a direct replication of Gerson's notion of adolescent baseline. What makes our study different from Gerson's is that this information was gathered when the women were aged seventeen or eighteen; we don't have to depend on their memories. In high school these young women were asked about their realistic aspirations for the relative priority of family and work in their lives. Possible responses ranged from:

1. Homemaking will be my major interest, and I will not want to work at all after getting married.
2. Homemaking will be my major interest, but I will want to work occasionally or work part-time.
3. Homemaking will be my major interest, but I will also want to work most of the time.
4. Work will be my major interest, but I will also want to have a family and be a homemaker.

Table 4.1. Means, Standard Deviations, and Correlations, N=1171

	1	2	3	4
Mean	22.94	1.22	2.43	23.31
Standard deviation	20.52	0.28	1.09	25.23
1 Respondent's hours worked per week	1.0			
2 Traditionality of sex role attitudes in 1966	-0.01	1.0		
3 Expected life interest (work or home?)	0.11***	-0.09**	1.0	
4 Realistic expected occupation	0.00	0.03	-0.07*	1.0
5 Don't mind competing with men	-0.08**	0.26***	-0.14***	0.01
6 Father's socioeconomic index	0.03	0.02	0.00	-0.12***
7 Father's educational attainment	0.01	0.00	0.04	-0.21***
8 Mother's educational attainment	0.04	0.01	0.04	-0.17***
9 High school grade point average	0.02	0.02	0.05	-0.26***
10 Parent's marriage intact during high school?	-0.03	0.02	-0.01	-0.06*
11 Respondent's educational attainment	0.08**	-0.01	0.14***	-0.39***
12 Number children in household in 1978	-0.18***	0.03	-0.16***	0.12***
13 Children younger than 6 in 1978?	-0.27***	0.05	-0.08**	0.02
14 Respondent ever divorced?	0.08**	0.02	0.02	0.08**
15 Husband's annual income (thousands of dollars)	-0.11***	-0.04	0.02	-0.04
16 Substantive complexity of occupation	0.12***	0.02	0.06*	-0.20***
17 Percentage male in occupation	0.18***	-0.01	0.07**	-0.08**
18 Mean career income growth (percentage)	0.05	0.01	0.00	-0.04
19 Mean career SEI growth (percentage)	0.00	0.01	-0.02	0.00
20 Number of promotions across jobs	0.13***	0.00	0.08*	0.02
21 Number of involuntary job shifts	0.00	-0.01	0.00	0.04
22 Months unemployed across jobs	0.02	0.00	0.02	0.03
23 Traditionality of sex role attitudes in 1979	-0.05	0.05	-0.04	0.08***
24 Define job as career?	0.23***	0.01	0.11***	-0.13***
25 Sample selection bias	-0.08***	0.05	-0.15***	0.28***

[a] Standard deviations inapplicable for dichotomous variables.

*$p < .05$; **$p < .01$; ***$p < .001$.

5	6	7	8	9	10	11	12
2.82	0.32	3.12	3.11	2.71	0.84	4.00	1.57
a	0.47	1.39	1.14	0.56	a	0.95	1.15
1.0							
-0.01	1.0						
-0.02	0.43***	1.0					
-0.02	0.23***	0.41***	1.0				
0.00	0.21***	0.28***	0.25***	1.0			
0.00	0.12***	0.01	0.02	0.09**	1.0		
-0.05	0.25***	0.41***	0.35***	0.43***	0.10***	1.0	
0.05	-0.13***	-0.16***	-0.17***	-0.16***	-0.05	-0.35***	1.0
0.04	-0.04	0.02	-0.02	-0.01	0.04	-0.06	0.55***
-0.02	-0.05	-0.10***	-0.09**	-0.12***	-0.08**	-0.19***	-0.05***
0.06*	0.08**	0.11***	0.04	0.07**	-0.01	0.06*	-0.04
-0.04	0.21***	0.27***	0.23***	0.33***	0.05	0.44***	-0.26
-0.10***	0.00	0.03	0.03	0.05	-0.02	0.06*	-0.13***
0.00	0.07**	0.08**	0.06*	0.01	0.03**	0.07	-0.07*
0.06*	0.02	-0.01*	-0.06	-0.01	-0.06*	-0.04	0.07**
-0.02	0.05	0.03	0.01	0.02	-0.04	-0.01	-0.09***
0.02	-0.05	0.00	0.02	-0.03	-0.01*	-0.06	-0.01
0.00	0.02	0.01	0.01	-0.02	0.06*	-0.01	-0.03
0.07*	-0.26***	-0.07**	-0.10***	-0.06*	-0.03	-0.18***	0.11***
-0.05	0.10***	0.13***	0.13***	0.15***	0.03	0.26***	
0.07**	-0.21***	-0.43***	-0.14**	-0.31***	0.28***	-0.66***	0.23***

Table 4.1. (*Continued*)

	13	14	15	16
Mean	0.57	0.20	20.11	13.44
Standard deviation	a	a	10.97	5.46

1 Respondent's hours worked
  per week
2 Traditionality of sex role attitudes
  in 1966
3 Expected life interest (work or
  home?)
4 Realistic expected occupation
5 Don't mind competing with men
6 Father's socioeconomic index
7 Father's educational attainment
8 Mother's educational attainment
9 High school grade point average
10 Parent's marriage intact during
  high school?
11 Respondent's educational attainment
12 Number children in household
  in 1978

	13	14	15	16
13 Children younger than 6 in 1978?	1.0			
14 Respondent ever divorced?	−0.17**	1.0		
15 Husband's annual income (thousands of dollars)	0.02	−0.02	1.0	
16 Substantive complexity of occupation	−0.07*	−0.08**	0.07**	1.0
17 Percentage male in occupation	−0.15***	0.07*	0.03	0.08**
18 Mean career income growth (percentage)	0.00	0.04	0.07**	0.02
19 Mean career SEI growth (percentage)	−0.01	0.04	−0.01	0.11***
20 Number of promotions across jobs	−0.06*	0.14***	0.02	0.07**
21 Number of involuntary job shifts	−0.05	0.08	−0.03	−0.13***
22 Months unemployed across jobs	−0.01	−0.01	0.01	−0.01
23 Traditionality of sex role attitudes in 1979	0.05	0.02	−0.04	−0.13***
24 Define job as career?	−0.14***	−0.01	0.08**	0.39***
25 Sample selection bias	0.10***	0.12	−0.05	−0.31***

17	18	19	20	21	22	23	24	25
32.06	15.29	28.52	1.69	0.27	0.67	2.34	0.44	1.28
31.13	48.55	57.34	2.60	0.62	4.11	1.81	a	0.29

1.0

0.03	1.0							
0.07*	0.07**	1.0						
0.10***	-0.01	-0.04	1.0					
0.07*	-0.01	0.04	0.05	1.0				
0.03	-0.01	0.03	0.03	0.15***	1.0			
-0.03	-0.02	0.01	-0.06*	-0.02	-0.05	1.0		
0.14***	0.07**	0.05	0.10***	-0.04	0.04	-0.03	1.0	
-0.06***	-0.03***	-0.05	-0.04	0.03	0.03	0.01***	0.23***	1.0

5. Work will be my major interest. I will not want to spend much effort in homemaking.

6. Work will be my only interest. I will not want to spend much effort in homemaking.

Most of these young women expected that homemaking would be their major interest and they would either not be employed after marriage or would work outside the home only occasionally or part-time. But there was a wide range of responses, from the 11.8 percent (N=138) who intended never to work after marriage to the 18.9 percent (N=221) who expected that homemaking would be their major interest but that they would also be employed most of the time.

Finally, we have two other measures for their realistic career aspirations as teenagers. We know what career they planned, and we coded that with a Duncan socioeconomic score, a measure of the social status (i.e., prestige level and pay) of the occupations to which these women aspired. Finally, the young women were asked about their willingness to compete with men in the occupational sphere. Sixty-three percent were neutral on this question. The mean answer was 2.86 on a 5-point scale.

With these questions, all asked of the respondents when they were teenagers, I believe that we obtained a clear sense of each woman's baseline orientation toward domesticity, based on values she internalized while growing up. These are strong measures for early gender-role socialization, the orientation that women bring to their adult lives.[2]

2. Three of the items used to measure socialization were replicated in the 1979 survey. Therefore, we used confirmatory factor analysis for all seven items to develop a scaled score. The statistical technique allowed us to correct for correlated errors in the measurement of the variables. (For more technical information see Risman, Atkinson, and Blackwelder 1994, 1998.)

Interactional measures. What happens at work and in one's family as an adult are the kinds of variables we included as interactional measures. Family context was measured by number of children in the household, presence of any child under the age of six, husband's income (in dollars per years), and whether the woman had ever been divorced. The average respondent had one or two children, and slightly more than half had a preschool-age child. The average husband's income was $20,000 in 1979 dollars, which is about double that in 1994 dollars (U.S. Department of Commerce 1995). Twenty percent of the women had been divorced.

A great deal of sociological research suggests, not surprisingly, that the presence of children in the home is negatively related to married women's labor-force participation (Cain 1966; Sweet 1973; Waite and Stolzenberg 1976; Smith-Lovin and Tickamyer 1978; Ewer, Crimmins, and Oliver 1979). We expect, then, that having more children—and children under six—would lead to fewer hours in paid work. Research (Waite and Stolzenberg 1976; McLaughlin 1982; Greenstein 1986) also has shown consistently that the higher a husband's income, the less likely his wife is to be in the full-time work force. We also guessed that having experienced divorce might leave women unwilling to depend solely on husbands for economic survival and would dispose them to remaining active in the labor force.

Experiences on the job can also be conceptualized as pulling one into or pushing one out of the labor force (Gerson 1985). Our measures of the work context include the following variables, which we suggest are pulls into the labor force: an increase in wages over all jobs held, an increase in the prestige of the jobs held, substantive complexity (or skill needed) of most recent job, number of promotions over one's career, and percentage of males in the respondent's current or most recent occupation (jobs with many men in them usually have the potential for more career growth and better current and future pay). Work variables that we considered pushes out of the labor force were number of times fired and number of months spent in nonvoluntary unemployment (time between being fired and finding another job). In this sample of women, the average wage growth in the thirteen-year period was was 15 percent. Most of the women worked in traditionally female occupations, had never been fired (78 percent), and had been out of work but looking for another job for less than a month (see table 4.1 for further details).

Adult orientation/labor force participation. We do not have a direct measure on what the women view as the optimum method of juggling paid work and family responsibilities as an adult. Therefore, we rely on a measure of their behavior: how many hours per week they spend in paid labor. The mean hours worked per week by the women in our sample was 22.94; some women had no labor-force participation, and a few worked 70 or more hours a week. We lacked the exact number of hours worked for 110 respondents (9 percent of the sample) who worked outside their home fewer than 25 hours per week and therefore estimated these women's hours at 12.5, the midpoint of the range. This is clearly a weakness in our data that we had no way to correct.

Other variables. In explaining what factors account for the hours that married women devote to labor force participation we must go beyond gender-role socialization and work and family contexts. Education, family background, and high school grades may affect women's choices as well.

In this study we assumed that education mediated between early socialization and adult experiences. That is, hopes and plans formed before high school graduation affect whether students go on to college. And higher education itself might shape a woman's decision about job choice and labor force participation in ways unforeseen in high school. Our measure of educational achievement is how many years of education each woman has completed. We also include statistical controls for parents' social status (measured by the prestige of the father's job and both parents' education), the respondent's grade point average in high school (taken from transcripts), and parents' marital status. Race was originally included as a background factor but was omitted because 97 percent of the respondents are white.

Findings

The easiest way to visualize the extent to which early socialization and plans made in adolescence shape women's lives is to return to the that format Gerson (1985) suggested. When we split the sample into two groups—those who plan to specialize in domesticity and those who do not—we can see how well the young women's goals predicted their eventual life patterns. The analyses show clearly that women who expected to be full-time wives and mothers were almost as likely to be employed full time (43 percent) as they were to be working only in their own homes (57 percent). Similarly, those who planned to remain in the labor force were almost as likely to be working only in their own homes (47 percent) as they were to have remained in the labor force (53 percent). Women are only slightly more likely to follow the paths they expect than not to. The effects of adolescent plans are real but not overwhelmingly powerful. Fifty-seven percent of those who expected to focus primarily on domestic work are at home full-time, but that still leaves 43 percent of those who planned to be homemakers working for pay full-time in their thirties. Similarly, 47 percent of those who planned to remain employed throughout their lives were working solely as homemakers at the time of the final survey. The explanation for women's choices clearly cannot be found in their gendered selves alone, but neither are their gendered plans irrelevant. Figure 4.1 indicates that attitudes formed in the teenage years are not particularly good predictors of eventual life patterns.

Figure 4.1. Adolescent and Adult Orientations to Family
Versus Paid Work: Empirical Results

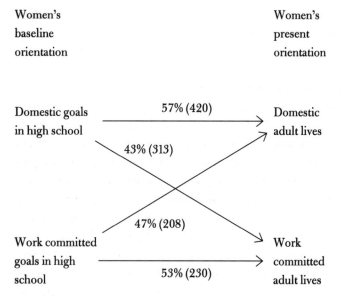

Women's
baseline
orientation

Women's
present
orientation

Domestic goals
in high school

57% (420)

43% (313)

47% (208)

Domestic
adult lives

Work committed
goals in high
school

53% (230)

Work
committed
adult lives

Further analysis (table 4.2, equation 1) indicates the same pattern: attitudes measured in adolescence have some influence on labor-force participation. (Again, while the equations are included here, an understanding of regression analysis is not necessary to follow the argument.) The variable with a statistical coefficient strong enough to be of real interest is respondents' life goals. Those girls who intended to remain interested in both employment and family roles do in fact work more hours per week than those whose primary goal was domesticity.

The other variable that was statistically significant but substantively weaker was the respondents' willingness to compete with men. Those teens who were less comfortable with the idea of competing with men spent somewhat less time in employment each week as adults. While these are statistically significant relationships (and thus indicate some importance to internalization of gendered selves), together the attitudes explain only 2 percent of the variation. In other words, if you know girls' goals and their feelings about competing with men, you will predict their adult life outcomes more accurately than if you did not have that information 2 percent of the time. Information about family background and educational achievement would not help any more in such predictions, for these variables were not related to how many hours women spent in paid labor.

We then tested the alternative strength of gendered selves versus the family and work contexts as predictors of these women's labor force participation.[3] The data in equation 5 show that adult family structure is indeed important for predicting married women's participation in the labor force. When women have a child under six they are considerably less likely to work long hours for pay. Women with preschoolers are likely to work almost ten fewer hours a week than others. Women married to well-to-do men are also less likely to spend long hours in the paid work force. For every additional $2,000 her husband made in 1979 dollars (about $4,000 in today's dollars) a wife in this sample is likely to work one half-hour less per week. Neither the total number of children at home nor whether the woman has been divorced was related to her current hours

3. The findings discussed in the text are based on ordinary least squares regression analyses. All analyses include a coefficient to control for sample selection bias. Control variables measuring the socioeconomic status of the respondent's background were added to the analyses in equation 2, and none are related to the dependent variable. (Again, for technical details see Risman, Atkinson, and Blackwelder 1994, 1997.)

Table 4.2. Predictors of Wives' Hours Worked, Controlling Sample Selection Bias

		1		2		3		4		5	
		b	B	b	B	b	B	b	B	b	B
Early attitudes	Traditionality of sex role attitudes	1.20	0.02	1.16	0.02	1.15	0.02	0.61	0.01	0.25	0.00
	Expected life interest (work or home?)	1.73***	0.09	1.71**	0.09	1.66**	0.09	1.38**	0.07	1.08*	0.06
	Realistic expected occupation	0.02	0.02	0.02	0.03	0.03	0.03	0.03	0.04	0.03	0.04
	Would not mind competing with men	-1.43*	a	-1.41*	a	-1.42*	a	-1.20	a	-0.64	a
Family of origin controls	Father's socioeconomic index			1.15	0.03	1.11	0.03	0.68	0.16	0.39	0.01
	Father's educational attainment			-0.81	-0.05	-0.81	-0.05	-0.76	-0.05	-0.38	-0.03
	Mother's educational attainment			0.87	0.05	0.67	0.04	0.53	0.03	0.40	0.02
	High school grade point average			-0.05	-0.00	-0.40	-0.01	-0.54	-0.01	-0.54	-0.01
	Parent's marriage intact during high school?			-0.75	a	-1.48	a	-1.60	a	-1.09	a
Education	Educational attainment					0.61	0.06	0.09	0.01	0.08	0.01
Adult attitudes	Traditionality of sex role attitudes							-0.12	-0.01	0.02	0.00
Family and work structure	Define job as a career							9.16***	a	7.06***	a
	Number children in household in 1978							0.55		0.03	

Group	Variable	Model 1 (b)	(β)	Model 2 (b)	(β)	Model 3 (b)	(β)	Model 4 (b)	(β)	Model 5 (b)	(β)
Pulls	Children younger than 6 in 1978?									-9.43***	a
	Ever been divorced?									1.12	a
	Husband's annual income (thousands of dollars)									-0.23***	-0.13
	Substantive complexity of occupation									0.17	0.05
	Percentage male in occupation									0.07***	0.11
	Mean career income growth (percentage)									0.02	0.05
	Mean career SEI growth (percentage)									-0.01	-0.02
Pushes	Number of promotions across jobs									0.63**	0.08
	Number of involuntary job shifts									-0.60	-0.02
	Months unemployed across jobs									0.04	0.01
	Sample selection bias weight	-4.67**	-0.07	-5.24*	-0.07	-3.01	-0.04	-2.56	-0.04	-1.20	-0.02
	Constant	26.79***		18.68*		23.04**		23.92*			
	Adjusted R-square	0.02		0.01		0.01		0.06		0.14	
	Change in F	27.73***		-1.97 n.s.		-0.12 n.s.		4.06***		2.52***	
	N of cases	1171		1171		1171		1171		1171	

[a] Standardized coefficients not presented for dichotomous variables.

*p < .05; **p < .01; ***p < .001.

in paid labor. These findings are consistent with most of the past sociological research (Collins and Coltrane 1995).

What is less well documented, however, is our finding that experiences at work, per se, are pulls into continuous labor-force participation. Women who work in occupations where males predominate are likely to work more hours; such jobs tend to offer higher status and better career growth and income potential. And while the relationship between the number of promotions over the thirteen years and the hours worked is weaker, it suggests a pattern of job characteristics that pull women into the labor force. Although we expected that jobs requiring more skill and offering greater variety of tasks would pull women into the labor force, they did not do so, at least directly. It is interesting to note, however, that the best predictor of whether a woman defines her paid work as a career is its substantive complexity, and that women who define paid work as a career are more likely to work more hours. Therefore, complex jobs tend to be defined as careers and, because of that definition, tend to increase women's labor-force participation.[4]

Neither of the variables we used to measure work experiences that might push women out of paid work (number of times fired and duration of nonvoluntary unemployment) was related to cur-

4. The analyses presented here actually require a slightly more complicated discussion. When the adult attitudinal items are added as intervening variables between gendered selves, work-family contexts, and labor force hours, the partitioning of variance jumps immediately. I have omitted that complication from the textual discussion in Chapter 4 because it is not directly relevant to the question posed here. The major change is that the attitudinal variable measured during adulthood—defining one's job as a career—increases the explained variance by 3 percent. Further analyses show that the strongest predictor of such an attitude is the substantive complexity of the job, further supporting the importance of work-family contexts to adult life choices. (For technical details see Risman, Atkinson, and Blackwelder 1994, 1998.)

rent labor-force hours. We did not find any work-related factors to help explain continued labor-force participation among the married women in our sample. Unfortunately, there was little variation in the answers to these questions, so finding an effect is statistically unlikely. Similarly, it may be that we did not have measures for other pushes out of the labor force, such as sex discrimination or harassment. Further research on these issues is clearly needed.

What happened when we added adult work and family structures to the analysis was fascinating: the accuracy of our predictions about a woman's participation in the labor force jumped from 6 percent (based on attitudes alone) to 14 percent (with information about adult interactional factors). Clearly the latter win out in any comparison of importance between gendered selves and adult experiences. The notion that childhood and adolescent socialization predicts adult outcomes because of internalized gendered selves is simply not supported by this longitudinal data. There is some evidence that attitudes toward family and work remain significant in adulthood, but they pale in comparison with experience in work and family contexts.

Conclusions

This research adds one more piece to my puzzle. I have posited that contextual-interactional factors are more immediate and stronger explanations for family patterns than is the existence of gendered selves. The women in this sample are particularly appropriate for exploring this theoretical question. They were raised before the labor-force participation of white married women was normatively accepted. While they were teenagers the second wave of the women's movement was born and feminist activism flourished. They were members of the first generation of white, middle-class, married women to enter the paid labor force in large numbers (Collins and Coltrane 1995). The nondomestic women in this sample are in some sense a naturally occurring experiment: women playing social roles for which they were not raised.

In our research we found that work and family contexts mattered much more than the gendered selves embedded in adolescent plans. But perhaps an even more important finding is that neither plans nor work and family experiences were particularly accurate predictors of women's labor-force participation. These analyses yielded statistically significant results and could explain approximately 14 percent of the variance, but that leaves 86 percent unexplained. We must keep this limitation in mind as we try to understand social life. People make choices and shape their own lives. Teenage attitudes do not predict women's choices as adults. But neither do their experiences at work or in their families tell us all we need to know. This reminds us that not only does society act on individuals but individuals make choices that shape society.

The next two chapters are about people who are consciously reshaping their own families and therefore the world itself. These are families in which gender is not used to organize the division of responsibilities. They come as close to living a post-gendered lifestyle as I have been able to find in contemporary society.

5

Playing Fair

Equity for the Educationally Elite

uch research on contemporary families focuses on the stalled revolution in most American homes: even when women spend as many hours in the paid labor force as their husbands do, they retain primary responsibility for homemaking and childrearing. The power of gender as a social structure is apparent in these typical families. To understand how and when the gender structure changes we must consider not only the typical family but also families who live on the cutting edge of social change. In this chapter we look at a statistically rare phenomenon — "fair" role-sharing families, those in which husbands and wives occupy breadwinner and nurturer roles equally.

There is a scarcity of research on couples who have redistributed family work equitably and without regard for the gendered division of responsibilities. There is a good reason for this dearth of research: such families are very rare in a statistical sense,[1] and social scientists prefer to study more mainstream families. All of the research in this field is made up of qualitative studies of recruited

1. There is some evidence (Blumstein and Schwartz 1983) that gay male and lesbian couples are much more likely to have an egalitarian division of labor in their households. I restrict my review of the literature to heterosexual married couples because they are more comparable to my respondents.

volunteer families because there are not enough such families to survey in a random sample. The research that does exist leads me to believe that there have been major changes in egalitarian families in the past two decades. The most striking change is that now some such families actually exist.

Findings from Past Research

The early studies (e.g., Rapaport and Rapaport 1972, Poloma 1971, Poloma and Garland 1971) found no examples of dual-career families in which the spouses were equally responsible for family work. In dual-career professional families the women were grateful to their husbands for allowing them the freedom to pursue their career goals. They did not expect their husbands to do more than help them out occasionally with family work. Studies of working-class dual-worker families (Komarovsky 1967; Rubin 1976) in the same era reported very traditional gender attitudes and family role distribution even though the women had to work for pay.

By the mid-1980s there were some couples who described themselves as sharing equally in the family work. Most of the studies from that era indicated, however, that while the couples were more equal than others, equality was more of an ideological commitment than a documentable reality (Kimball 1983; Hertz 1986; Russell 1983). In several studies (Kimball 1983; Ehrensaft 1987; Haas 1980, 1982) the husbands and wives were often veterans of the social justice movements of the 1960s and 1970s and were ideologically committed to nonsexist, nonracist, nonviolent childrearing. They were educated and often were working in human services or education. The sample reporting the most egalitarian behaviors was the also the sample least likely to have children (Haas 1980, 1982). Ehrensaft was particularly adept at identifying and explaining the discrepancies between the ideology and the reality of her respondents' daily lives. The men were committed to doing their share at home and reluctant to assume the entire responsibility for supporting the family. The wives were enthusiastic about their relatively egalitarian marriages. Yet in three important ways gender emerged as an important explanation of differences between fathers and mothers, Ehrensaft reported: wardrobe management, worrying, and scheduling. For example, the women usually bought the children's clothes and made sure they looked presentable, even when the father actually dressed the child. Similarly, the mothers usually managed the household schedule and worried about balancing activities.

Other studies report similar findings (Hertz 1986; Russell 1983). In a study of corporate couples Hertz found agreement that all household and childrearing should be split equally, and she found that most of it indeed was. But the ultimate responsibility for household management still fell to the wives, even if in these high-earning couples that meant hiring and supervising the help. A similar finding was reported by Russell in his study of "shared caregiver" couples. Russell's Australian sample was larger and much more demographically varied than any of the American samples discussed thus far. He compared 71 families in which husbands shared caregiving at least equally with their wives with 145 traditional mother-at-home families. Half the fathers in the "shared caregivers" group were stay-at-home dads, however, so the men in this sample are not strictly comparable to the American samples discussed above or to the men in my sample. Indeed, this difference is quickly apparent in the data itself, with the fathers reporting many of the same complaints that housewives have voiced for decades — not being appreciated and being starved for adult companionship. But they also report that they value the increased quality of their relationships with their children. What is relevant to this discussion, however, is that even though half the fathers in this sample were specializing in child care and homemaking as their primary work, the mothers *still* usually retained ultimate responsibility for child-rearing.

In nearly every family in samples collected through the mid-1980s, husbands and wives attributed their differences in attitudes and responsibilities to individual personality traits. Yet the pattern was clear across studies: women remained responsible for keeping the domestic ship afloat—seeing what needed to be done, scheduling it, and making sure that children were presentable. These couples were sharing labor more or less equally, but not responsibility.

In the late 1980s new studies showed how families were beginning to change. Coltrane (1989, 1990) studied a sample of households in which slightly more than half of the couples (twelve of twenty) seemed to be sharing equally both labor and management in their homes; the rest described themselves as sharing equally but fall into the pattern described above, with fathers "helping" a great deal but not sharing equally. The families in Coltrane's studies were not nearly as driven ideologically as those in the earlier samples. The parents were sharing equally because they were committed to quality nonsexist childrearing. Both parents chose jobs with flexible schedules, and both made children their first priority. By this time, however, there was a culturally available gender-equity ideology for these couples to use implicitly if not explicitly in justifying their choices. In an even more recent study, Blaisure and Allen (1995) looked at ten couples in which both husband and wife had identified themselves as feminists before their marriage; two had actually shared the family work while raising young children. By the 1990s, gender structure had changed enough to allow some gender-equity oriented men and women to negotiate egalitarian marriages.

The largest and most ambitious study of egalitarian marriages appeared in 1994 (Schwartz). In 1983, Pepper Schwartz and Philip

Blumstein published a mammoth study of different kinds of relationships in *American Couples*. Schwartz returned nearly a decade later to interview the few heterosexual role-sharing couples from the earlier study. Her sample snowballed to the friends and acquaintances of the original group; eventually she interviewed fifty-six couples whom she labeled as living in "peer marriages." Her bases for including couples in the sample as peer marriages were more intuitive than formal. There were, however, four commonalities that appeared to be characteristics of peer marriages: the division of household work and responsibility stayed within a 40/60 range; both spouses believed that they had equal influence over important and disputed decisions; both partners felt that they had equal control over family economic resources and equal access to discretionary spending; and both persons' work was given equal weight in the couple's life plans.

One unexpected but interesting finding was that the men were usually mid-rank professionals with incomes too low to encourage their wives to remain outside the labor force or to make the women's salary unimportant. There were some "power" couples, in which both partners had successful and consuming careers, but they were in the minority. Nearly all of the couples were in their mid-twenties to early fifties. Schwartz's research improves on previous studies because she gathered data from peer couples and from twenty-two "near-peers" (i.e., couples in which both partners were employed but the husbands did not equally share household labor) and from twenty-two male-dominated (i.e., traditional) couples with a well-defined gender-based division of labor.

Schwartz reports that there are distinct rewards and costs in peer marriages. The major reward is the primacy of the relationship and the importance of intimate friendship to the couple. These couples are best friends, committed partners, and they find each other irreplaceable. The depth and quality of their relationship is the driving force in their lives. But such intensive commitment to each other and to sharing equally has its costs. Friends and family are still unlikely to be supportive of this kind of marriage, particularly for the man. In traditional marriages women balance work and childrearing, usually by forgoing jobs incompatible with parenting. In the peer couples both partners must make career choices that allow them to parent together, giving up opportunities for advancement that require extensive travel or overtime. It can be painful for the women and men in these marriages to watch colleagues advance faster in their careers even though they have given family responsibilities a priority. Peer partners also become so close emotionally that they may end up acting like friends rather than lovers in bed. Schwartz suggests that their very closeness can trigger an incest taboo based on overfamiliarity. These couples must work to keep eroticism in their deep friendship.

The "Fair Family" Study

I wanted to know more about gender dynamics in families headed by peers. With a team of research colleagues I spent an entire semester writing and revising interview formats for peer couples and their children.[2] (Data techniques used with the children are discussed in the next chapter.) This was particularly challenging

2. These data were collected over the four years by a team of researchers. Interviewers were Stephen Blackwelder, Sandra Godwin, Steven Jolly, Kristen Myers, Jammie Price, Margaret Stiffler, Danette Johnson-Sumerford, and myself. Johnson-Sumerford handled the complex tasks of screening volunteers and scheduling interviews. Myers did all the organizational work necessary to create the qualitative coding scheme using Ethnograph computer software. Blackwelder organized the quantitative surveys and instruments. The research was a remarkable team effort. It would have been impossible without the financial support of the College of Humanities and Social Sciences at North Carolina State University.

because we wanted to include children as young as four and as old as eighteen in our study. Data collection with adults included a life history interview; focused questions about their relationships, childrearing, and paid work; and card sorting exercises to assess the details of household labor more accurately. An earlier discussion of these couples can be found in Risman and Johnson-Sumerford (1998).

Our hardest challenge was to find "fair" families. We had very specific criteria for inclusion in this sample because we wanted to make sure that we were studying couples who "play fair," not second-shift (near-peer) families, in which women worked for pay and did more than their share at home. We asked everyone we knew for referrals. We advertised in every PTA newsletter in Wake County, North Carolina, and in the staff publication of our university. We posted signs or mailed fliers to every day-care center in the city of Raleigh and to many libraries and fitness centers. We posted ads on grocery-store bulletin boards. We also recruited via networks in the Women's Studies programs of Duke, University of North Carolina at Chapel Hill, and North Carolina State University. We advertised in local feminist group newsletters (National Organization for Women and the National Abortion Rights Action League) and in newsletters of local churches and synagogues. We had plenty of referrals from people we knew and a number of responses from people who saw the advertisements or fliers and wanted to participate. But then the trouble began.

The first stage of data collection was a very short survey designed to separate the second shift (near-peer) and more traditional couples from those in which the husbands and wives shared equitably. Our standards were not too stringent. We used criteria similar to those used by Schwartz (1994): the division of labor had to be within a 40/60 range, each spouse had to believe that both partners were equally responsible for earning a living and caring for their children, and each had to believe that the relationship was "fair." In order for any family to be included in this study, both the husband and wife had to believe that the family was fair to himself or herself, and if any "unfairness" was reported it had to be in gender atypical directions (e.g., the husband did more than half the cleaning). The family also had to include a child between the ages of four and eighteen living in the home. We sent questionnaires only to families that had been screened on the telephone and who had told us that they shared equally in the work of earning a living and rearing their children.[3]

The Sample

We sent a survey to the seventy-five families who had volunteered to participate and seemed eligible based on our screening conversation. The survey worked well: only once did our screening device let through a family in which the woman did more than her share. The problem was, however, that this screened group of seventy-five families yielded us only fifteen who met our criteria for inclusion. Only one of five families who identified themselves as equitable on the telephone, or 20 percent, actually shared the household labor in a 40/60 or better split, agreed that they shared equally the responsibility for breadwinning and childrearing, and felt that their relationship was fair. That alone tells us much about the strength of our gender structure for creating inequitable marriage. Yet I do not want to discredit the tendency toward egalitarianism in the rest of the families who volunteered to participate. The husbands and

3. The data presented in this book are drawn entirely from the fair family interviews and home observations. Findings based on the larger survey sample and the quantitatively analyzed card-sorting exercises are not presented here. We simply gathered too much information to present it in this one chapter. My colleagues are writing journal articles based on these data as well.

wives in the families we did not include in our sample were trying to share equally—they were challenging the gender structure. Even if they were not entirely successful they clearly are part of the massive social change that feminism has inspired. Still, as a social analyst, I find it remarkable that the taken-for-granted nature of female responsibility for family work hides a gendered division of labor even from many fair-minded couples themselves.

The fifteen families who met our criteria were educationally elite. More than half of the parents (eight men and nine women) had a Ph.D. or an M.D. Another eight parents had master's degrees (usually in education or business). Three fathers and one mother had a bachelor's degree only, and one mother had never completed college. These families were not necessarily rich, as many had given up high-paying jobs or occupations in order to care for their children equally. Others were college professors, a group with notoriously high educational attainment relative to their incomes. Nevertheless, these were the only families who met our criteria. The question is why?

This may partly reflect our local population. It is a widely believed myth that the triangle of cities in North Carolina—Chapel Hill, Durham, and Raleigh—has more doctorates per capita than any other part of the country. It is true that with three major universities, several colleges, and a research park in the center of the triangle there are a many highly educated people in our region. But there are many less educated persons in our region as well, and some of them sent in questionnaires that were eliminated because the couple did not really play fair. My own explanation is that women in our society lack the clout and or self-assurance to seek a peer marriage unless they are highly educated, income-producing professionals. Although higher education and the ability to earn a good living cannot create a peer marriage, they do seem to be necessary conditions. The women in our sample were self-assured, strong-willed, committed to their work, and had eagerly sought parenthood. College—and for most of these women, graduate school—is where they developed the human capital that allows them to earn incomes equivalent to their spouse's income. College is also where some women and men are introduced to feminist ideals. These women not only believe in women's equality but they take the ideology so much for granted that they rarely mention it unless pushed to do so. Such highly educated, feminist women tend to marry equals, so their husbands are also highly educated, income-producing professionals. The men in this sample were perhaps more atypical than their wives. They tended to be easygoing, family-centered, and secure enough to negotiate nontraditional roles. They were willing to forgo the advantages of male privilege that usually accompany marriage. My guess is that many more women would choose egalitarian marriage if they could, but the pool of men interested in actual equality is quite small. Another unusual pattern was the number of couples in the same sort of work: three academic couples in the same fields (two even in the same departments) and two couples in similar fields but different workplaces. Another pattern quickly became obvious: many of these wives (six of the fifteen) either earned more than their husbands or worked in more prestigious occupations. Only two husbands outranked their wives in this way. The norm, however, was for the spouses to hold equally prestigious jobs and earn comparable incomes. All of the families were white.

These couples' egalitarian outlooks are mirrored in the variety of surnames they adopted. In only half of the families (eight of fifteen) had the wife assumed her husband's name, and in these families the children bore his name also. In two of the families each parent retained her or his name, and the children's surnames were hyphenated. In three families the mother and father retained their birth names, but the children carried only the father's name. In one family the mother hyphenated her name (by adding her husband's after her own), but the child used only the father's surname. And finally, in one family, each parent retained her or his own birth name, and the children carried the mother's name. In the following analyses, however, I follow the simple rule of giving each family a pseudonym and using that code name for all members of the family. Although it does not faithfully represent the family's naming policy this rule will help the reader to keep track of which husbands and wives, parents and children, are in the same family. To protect the respondents' anonymity, identifying characteristics such as names, occupations, and workplaces have been changed. Table 5.1 displays the family information.

Analytic Framework

To analyze how the gender structure has influenced these families and to what degree they have managed to transform it, I used a conceptual framework offered by Connell in *Gender and Power* (1987). He argues that an adequate theory of gender structure requires a focus on external constraint beyond the voluntarism of sex roles. In the theoretical language I have proposed in this book, this means that internalized gendered selves are not powerful enough explanations for the continued reliance on gender to organize responsibilities within the family or elsewhere. Instead, we must look at both the interactional and institutional levels of analysis for a complete structural understanding. Connell also argues, as do I, that the external constraints embedded in institutional arrangements cannot alone be a complete structural analysis because human beings have the ability to remake their environments, to reflexively reject the worlds they inherit, and to transform them. Connell writes that "to describe structure is to specify what it is in the situation that constrains the play of practice. . . . since human action involves free invention . . . and human knowledge is reflexive, practice can be

Table 5.1. List of Fair Families

Family Name	Children
Cary	5-year-old boy
Cody	7-year-old girl
	4-year-old boy
Cross	6-year-old girl
	4-year-old girl
Germane	11-year-old girl
Green	6-year-old girl
Oakley	10-year-old boy
	4-year-old girl
Potadman	17-year-old boy
	15-year-old boy
	12-year-old boy
Pretzman	8-year-old boy
	3-year-old boy
Relux	6-year-old girl
	4-year-old boy
Staton	9-year-old boy
	6-year-old boy
Stokes	10-year-old girl
Sykes	9-year-old girl
Trexler	4-year-old boy
	baby girl
Valt	3-year-old girl
	baby girl
Woods	10-year-old boy
	baby boy

turned against what constrains it; so structure can be deliberately the object of practice" (95).

I agree with Connell that many structural analyses of gender have been overly deterministic. Structural conditions channel possible actions but do not preordain the outcomes. Change is historically uneven and is the result of internal contradictions between structural arrangements (e.g., when the institutional, interactional, and individual levels of the gender structure contradict each other) as well as of the conscious struggle of the people involved. In Connell's theory the gender regime of each social institution (such as the family) can be analyzed structurally by attending to three arenas: labor, control, and cathexis. *Labor* refers to who does what kind of work and how much society values it. Labor issues include discrimination in wages, sex segregation of jobs, the division of housework and child care, and the relative time and effort devoted to different kinds of work. *Control* refers to who has authority in any given context and how it is expressed. The means of social control used to circumscribe behavior range from ridicule to the threat of violence to incarceration. *Cathexis* refers to the emotional aspects of daily relations, including sexuality, trust, jealousy, and desirability. The analysis of cathexis includes probing the intensity of emotional connections and determining who has the responsibility for and work of keeping feelings alive and in check. I have analyzed the data here according to Connell's framework. An earlier adaptation of this framework to these data can be found in Risman and Johnson-Sumerford (1998).

Labor

This sample, by definition, has little variation in the distribution of household labor and in the number of hours each parent devotes to paid work. But stories about how the families got to such a shared place provide much information about the alternative paths to peer marriages.

Four relationships leading to an equitable division of household labor were identified: dual-career couples, dual-nurturer couples, post-traditionals, and those pushed by external circumstances. In dual-career marriages both partners had always been interested in their own career growth and success, as well as in co-parenting their children. Dual-nurturer couples were more child-centered than work centered, with both parents organizing their work lives almost exclusively around their parental responsibilities. Post-traditional couples had spent at least part of their adult lives in husband-breadwinner and wife-nurturer roles and had consciously rejected that model. And two couples had been pushed into "fair" relationships by circumstances beyond their control. In one such family, the wife's job was the organizing principle for the family's life because she earned nearly twice as much as her husband, who was not very career oriented. In the other family the wife's chronic illness was at least partly responsible for the husband's domestic labor.

Dual-Career Couples

The most common route to peer marriage—and the one I had expected because it mirrors my own experience—was the partnership of two career-oriented professionals who both held egalitarian values. Two-thirds of the couples in this study (ten of fifteen) divided their labor "fairly" because both partners were career and equity oriented. Both parents compromised work goals to balance family and career priorities, but both remained committed to their careers as well as their childrearing responsibilities. In all but one of these ten couples, both partners had always studied or worked full-time, shared household responsibilities before parenthood, and never considered any childrearing style other than co-parenting.

In one couple, the wife had stayed home for a year after the birth of their daughter while her husband held a temporary position; she remembered the experience as atypical and miserable. She was lonely and unhappy with no work other than mothering. These are families in which both husband and wife simply assume that a fulfilling life involves both paid and family work. No husband or wife articulated, without some probing, an ideological justification for this assumption; they simply had adopted the culturally available feminist view on equality as their own taken-for-granted reality.

A remarkable finding is the absence of gender expectations used as a basis for organizing labor. Not one of these couples mentioned that they had ever considered that the wife devote herself exclusively to family work. No husband or wife complained about consistently doing more than a fair share of housework, nor did the men wish that their wives were more traditionally domestic. Only two of the ten dual-career couples reported any serious conflict over division of labor, usually long in the past. Often the couples never had negotiated at all. One mother, a mathematician married to a public policy analyst explained,

> We didn't tend to do the "You'll do half of the
> time, I'll do half of the time." We tended to divide
> tasks up, [decide] who would do them. So Karl
> liked to cook. He cooked for himself before we ever
> married. I didn't cook for myself at all before we
> were married. I ate out or in the cafeteria where I
> worked, so we didn't really have to adapt ourselves
> in that way. If he had wanted to share the cooking
> because he didn't much like it, I probably would've
> divided it in some way, half and half, but we tended
> to sort jobs. He didn't like to do laundry, I like to
> do laundry. I didn't mind cleaning up, I do the

> cleaning up . . . the dishes and wiping up counters
> and stuff. So we found a way that we considered
> equitable . . . but we did talk about it and we did
> consciously do it.

In another household the family tried to divide the cooking 50:50 but quickly reverted to sorting tasks by preference—here the mother cooked and father cleaned up afterward.

The absence of gender as a criterion for determining labor is evident in the following quotation as well. In this household the philosopher father has considerably more flexibility in his work schedule than the mother, who works in management in a multinational corporation. When asked how they organized tasks this husband replied,

> I think within a year after we got married Pam got
> her degree and started working full time. Since
> then I have taken on the majority of domestic labor.
> I have never had a grudge. Occasionally I will say,
> "It would be nice if you did a little more." I have
> never really felt exploited. If we were both work-
> ing the same kind of strict hours and one of us
> did the majority then I would expect one of us to
> raise their hand and say this is not fair. My hours
> are flexible so it's not a big deal for me to throw a
> load of laundry in the washer or dryer while I am
> grading papers.

The one way that gender did manifest itself in the family labor of dual-career couples was that the wives sometimes came to the relationship with higher standards of cleanliness. But unlike more traditional families, these couples did not use this difference to justify an extra burden for the wife. Rather, differing standards were seen as a problem to be worked out equitably. This psychoanalyst married to a real estate salesman explained,

> Sam had been a bachelor for a long time. He was thirty-five when we got married, so he knew how to do dishes and laundry and he knew how to cook one thing. He did things like keep his dirty, greasy garbage in a paper bag under the sink so that the entire sink was so greasy. . . . After trying to clean it I had to paint it. I did teach him how to use plastic. So there were a lot of things that he just didn't notice or care about initially which he has now incorporated into his routine. It's not that he's a man and doesn't do that stuff, it's just that he's absent-minded, and at this point he's a lot more concerned about certain neatness than I am. He'll vacuum periodically; I don't. I don't like the noise. He's the vacuumer and I tolerate mess more than he does.

In only one household were there current discussions and negotiations about household labor. A free-lance editor married to a professor reported ongoing negotiations about the standards of household cleanliness. But he had reconceptualized the problem in standard feminist language: "I know the thing that men have the hardest time learning how to do is noticing that there is dust. Men can't see dust. Men don't know what dust is. I still don't see. I don't know it's there. I know that . . . the nirvana of nonsexist male development is [noticing] dust. If I get to the dust stage, I'll know that I've really made it."

The conceptualization of varying opinions as problems to be negotiated and solved differs dramatically from the strategies reported in Hochschild's (1989) study of second-shift couples. When couples subscribe to traditional gender norms a husband who helps out at home is highly appreciated by his wife because he is doing more than expected; she owes him in their "economy of gratitude." When couples profess to believe in gender equality, however, husbands get no extra credit for doing housework; it is simply presumed that they should.

Dual-Nurturer Couples

Two couples were dual nurturers, oriented to home, family, and lifestyle rather than career. They worked for pay so that they could spend time together and with their families. Only one of these couples was unequivocally dual nurturing, however. In the Woods family, neither parent has worked full-time consistently for years, and neither wants to do so. The father, an aspiring sculptor, works half-time as an editor; the mother is an accountant who sees clients three days a week. They try to organize their work schedules so that both are not working during the same day, even though their baby is in day care and their other child is in school and after-school programs. They feel that the evenings are too hectic if both arrive home at the same time after a full day away. Their work schedules and choice of jobs have varied with family needs. In many ways this looked like a home with two mothers in that neither parent was strongly attached to the labor force. This couple was particularly focused on the quality of their lives rather than material acquisition or career development. Yet the couple did not appear to be suffering economically from their career decisions. They lived in a modern, energy-efficient home they had designed themselves. Original artwork, painting, and pottery were in evidence in their rural, picturesque setting.

Post-Traditional Couples

The third route to a division of equitable labor was dissatisfaction with more traditional arrangements. Two of the couples in this study were post-traditional families. In the case of the Germanes, both partners' previous marriages had been organized around traditional gendered expectations and responsibilities. The woman stated clearly that she had left a previous marriage because her husband did not meet her needs for an equal partner. She had been married to a career diplomat and had moved every three years of her adult life. As a bookkeeper in government service she found it easy to relocate, and she had never been unemployed more than three months in her entire working life because of the "work ethic I grew up with." Paid work was important to her sense of self. When asked about her maternity leave, she answered, "I do feel that three months out of work—I don't care who I'm taking care of—is a lot of time." She cut back her work to thirty-two hours a week during her daughter's infancy, but only because her husband was on an assignment that involved much travel. Her current husband, who also had been a diplomat, had returned to school for another college degree when their daughter was in the early elementary grades. Ms. Germane enthusiastically recalled, "I liked the role reversal when he was the housewife. . . . He walked [our daughter] to school and I swear he knew every lady in the school. . . . He became a PTA mom." Both husband and wife reported having always shared work equally; the wife was very much aware that they seemed to share things "more in the middle" than other people. Even now that the husband is again working full-time in business management the couple continue to share labor equally. Both husband and wife had experienced less satisfying relationships, and they were, in Schwartz's (1994) language, very deep friends. Both wanted to keep things fair to protect their precious friendship.

The other post-traditional couple had renegotiated their

gender-based roles when the youngest of their three boys entered kindergarten. It took this family three to four years to transform a decade-long male-breadwinner/female-homemaker pattern into a fair relationship. The wife was clearly the moving force behind this transformation. Ms. Potadman told us about her resentment at spending Saturdays doing housework after she returned to nursing full-time. Eventually her family—at her urging—divided the household tasks with a scheduling system. The mother explains it this way: "I had the idea, let's just list the tasks and we'll divide them up, and whenever he [her husband] gets his done, he gets them done." This wife still holds primary responsibility for the scheduling sessions. The entire family talked at length about the scheduling charts they used: each son cooked one day a week, the mother twice, and the father once, with dinner out every Friday. The sons were assigned cleanup tasks on days they did not cook.

The mother seemed to use the work of scheduling to join together family members in a common concern. Although there are five members in this family, half of the schedule itself is in the mother's handwriting. In addition, observations in the home showed that even though the children decide what they'll cook on their nights as chef, the mother periodically offers help and advice. Even though they all abide by and create the calendar, the mother gets them to think about events through the scheduling ritual. The mother seemed to spend a great deal of energy maintaining this arrangement. The father seemed to go along with it because his wife had a very persuasive personality, and his own ideological orientation valued justice and doing his share. The father was also considerably more relaxed and easygoing than his wife.

Couples Pushed into Sharing

The final route to a fair relationship was to be pushed by external forces. In one family the wife had a considerably better-paying job and a much less flexible schedule. In another family the wife was chronically ill. In both of these families gender equality was the conceptual framework that helped them make sense of their lives. In many ways they saw these external constraints in gender-neutral terms. In the Cody family the wife earned two-thirds of the household income. The husband had been passed over for a promotion that he had expected, and quit his job and changed careers. Mr. Cody was no longer work-focused and was pleased to have a flexible schedule. He enjoyed the freedom of owning a small business without the economic burden of supporting the family on his income.

> When we decided that we were going to have children Marilyn's job situation was such that . . . she worked in a reasonably structured environment, and in that case you can't take time off to bring somebody to gymnastics and, you know, go to the school for plays and . . . give parties and do that kind of stuff. So we made a decision that I would do that, and what it does basically is it takes me out of, you know, being the high-powered career person and, you know, . . . I just do something that brings in some money, and [parenting] gives me satisfaction that I can do it.

In the Stokes family, in which the wife was chronically ill, the husband similarly explained, in remarkably gender-free language, that his wife did not do much domestic work: "Because of her work schedule and because of her physical limitations, I do almost all of the cleaning because it gets just physically difficult for her to do that." His wife could not drive, so this father also did all the car pooling for the daughter's activities as well as all the shopping.

It is important to acknowledge explicitly that none of these "ideal types" is pure. At least one dual-career couple could perhaps have been categorized as dual nurturers. One couple, the Sykeses, had given up more lucrative jobs to teach high school for the flexibility to be better parents to their daughter and to have a higher quality of family life. Both had adapted well to their new work environments and were once again interested in career growth, both moving toward administrative responsibilities.

Another caveat about this sample: in all but two of these fifteen families paid help was employed for some cleaning tasks. The usual scenario was for a cleaning company to come in twice a month to do the vacuuming, dusting, and bathrooms. These couples had the luxury of not having to split the most odious homemaking jobs. Still, both husbands and wives report that they shared the work even before they had housecleaners. Most families began hiring help when their children were born. Nearly every family came to the same decision: weekends were better spent in family leisure activities than on housework. And these families were privileged enough economically to buy themselves out of nearly a day per month of household labor.

In summary, not one of the thirty parents interviewed even suggested that the husband's paid work was more important than the wife's. In fact, four of these families had moved to North Carolina because of the wife's work, and not one husband or wife mentioned this as unusual. Another four had relocated to North Carolina because of the husband's job; in two of these families the wife's ability to transfer was mentioned as a prerequisite for relocation. Another three families relocated because both partners found positions in the area. The other four couples were living there when they met. Not one of the thirty parents suggested that caring for their babies was or should have been more the mother's responsibility. Not one believed that housework should be the wife's responsibility, although half did admit to conflict at some point in their relationship about standards of cleanliness. It is to how conflict is negotiated and power exercised in fair families that I now turn.

Control

Control refers to the cultural lines of authority and coercion, the status differential between men and women that is at the root of our gender structure. There are countless overt and subtle means by which male privilege is constructed in daily life. Women's fear of rape constrains their mobility in ways that men never experience. Fear of ridicule and social disapproval keeps women, from girlhood on, worried about their weight and physical attractiveness. The wage gap and sexual harassment in the workplace also reinforce male dominance. The normative belief that husbands should head the household also explicitly reinforces dominance and provides cultural authority for men to control their wives. Similarly, the continuing expectation that wifehood involves domestic service is yet another way that male privilege and female subordination is re-created in daily life. While such daily inequity appears to pale in comparison with fear of rape, the expectation that women provide domestic services to husbands and primary care for children not only creates inequitable marriages but also disadvantages women in the world of work.

Yet there are families—fair families—in which the marital control issues that reinforce male privilege appear to be moot. These women and men are both pioneers in and beneficiaries of the women's liberation movement. Yet given the history of male dominance, we would be remiss if we simply accepted a check on a paper-and-pencil survey as an adequate measure of the balance of power and control in these couples.

We therefore explored these issues with interview questions about how decisions were made about where to live, how to discipline children, how to organize housework, and how to allocate leisure time. In nine of fifteen couples we found no evidence that either member had more power or influence in the marriage. In six of these nine couples, no matter how much we probed we simply could not elicit any hint that the couple had any areas of active conflict. When asked about the worst thing in their marriage or the one thing they would change, these couples mentioned scarcity of time to enjoy each other's company. This is Ms. Cross's response to a question about the very worst thing in her marriage: "I wish I had more time with him. Alan and I don't get to do things together alone — go alone for walks, repaint the house, refinish furniture."

In the other three couples without any power imbalance, either husband or wife, and sometimes both, talked openly about areas of conflict but did not imply that either partner had more influence in resolving such issues. These couples reported some conflict about standards of cleanliness, yet the tone of the discussions seemed to be about accommodation rather than about winning or losing the battle. One father, who did most of the housework in his family, explained, "Our conflicts have been mainly over what constitutes an acceptable standard of cleanliness. I'm content to let things get dustier than Cary is. She gets much more bothered by the dust and the dirt than I do. I don't think on the full spectrum of humanity that I am . . . at an extreme, but I'm more willing to let things go than she is."

In the other six couples the wives seemed to have more influence. These wives are outgoing, assertive, organized, and ambitious. The husbands all are introverted, quiet, and low-key. When asked how their relationship became marriage-oriented, Ms. Relux answered, "I intended to finish my residency and go back up north because I had done a year of internship in Connecticut and it was such a relief to get away from very southern men. When I met Sam I really liked him and I wanted to get to know him and probably marry him, and I kept trying to call him." The husband's interview, conducted in a different room by a different team member, confirmed the story: "Well, I was fortunate to meet Nelly and for whatever reason I was immediately the man of her dreams. I'm not sure why."

Ms. Relux reinforced our view that she was the mover and shaker in this relationship with her response to questions about the couple's decision to marry and have children: "Just as I had to drag him into having children, I had to drag and push him into getting married. . . . He's a stick in the mud. He is very happy for everything to be the way that it is always. It's easier." Her husband told us the same thing: "I've been dragged along through each stage of life."

The following replies from the Greens also suggest that the husbands in this group sometimes acquiesced to their wives' needs, in this case the demand for equity in the responsibility for household labor and not merely in the time spent. Ms. Green told us: "In the beginning it was really hard and we argued about it all the time. I had to lower my standards and Stan had to raise his. He had to learn to recognize that certain things had to be done in the house and that he could take that responsibility. He was willing, he was just ignorant." Mr. Green told the same story: "It was definitely a process of Roberta having to complain and me having to shape up."

Perhaps Mr. Potadman best articulated how the wives and husbands in these six couples differed. He described how their relationship had started: "She was very vivacious and outgoing. . . . I guess those are qualities I feel missing in myself—enthusiasm and things like that. So I guess I was drawn to that."

The pattern of strong women and quiet, adaptable men—evident in these six couples—is decidedly different from the majority of fair families, in which the husbands and wives had more similar personalities. In no couple did the husband seem to hold more power than his wife.

Although these couples live in a world in which men, as a class, have more power, property, and prestige than women do (Reskin and Padavic 1994), they have managed to create marital relationships that honor gender equality. The women have many advantages at their disposal: they are economically independent, so marriage is not a route to bed and board. And the men have privileges as well: their paid work is not the sole support of the family, so they are free to explore second careers and to choose lower-paying, more enjoyable work, as they can and do depend on their wives to shoulder at least half of the breadwinning responsibilities. But I believe that the major reason power and control issues seem so peripheral to the daily experiences of these couples is that these husbands and wives are deep friends. Ms. Sykes is articulate about this: "We really communicate well, we are both supportive and good listeners for each other. I will tell Peter things about myself that I won't tell anybody else. There is a level of trust and intimacy that is unequaled in any other relationship I have." These deep friendships, and the structural equality of equivalent jobs and pay that undergirds them, make the household division of labor fair. But household labor is hardly all there is to family life; the realm of emotion and intimacy is even more important to satisfied spouses.

Cathexis

Connell's (1987) theory about cathexis is that the social structure manifests itself in intimate relationships, in the construction of sexual desire and the intensity of emotional attachments. Cathexis is part of the social structure because beliefs and emotions are constraints on everyday practices. The gender structure patterns our desire for intimacy, sexual and otherwise. Historically, the very opposition of masculinity and femininity was incorporated into the definition of heterosexual attraction. Schwartz reported that the peer couples in her study faced a need to rediscover pathways to the erotic because in American society eroticism is often based on difference and domination, something lacking in peer marriages.

In our study we explored issues revolving around cathexis by focusing on the emotional connection between the parents, the intensity of emotional bonds between each parent and the children, and the extent to which personality difference existed within these marriages. We did not probe into these couples' sexual relationships, but some of the parents volunteered information about sex.

No single pattern emerged in terms of these couples' relationships except for the one already mentioned: in nearly every couple both partners mentioned spontaneously that the spouse was his or her best friend, irreplaceable and precious. Only in two couples, both among those pushed into fair relationships by external factors, did we sense any marital dissatisfaction. It is certainly possible that the quality of these relationships is simply the result of a volunteer bias; perhaps only couples who are this satisfied in their marriages agree to participate in a research project as intrusive as ours. But I do not think so. In Hochschild's (1989) research on dual-worker families in which wives shoulder more than their fair share, many of the wives spoke clearly and forcefully about the resentment and emotional estrangement created by inequity.

Beyond the general report of very high marital satisfaction among our respondents, however, there was no pattern. Three very different emotional types emerged. The first type was families in which there is almost a traditional emotional relationship: the women are more emotionally sensitive, and this manifests itself in the marriage and their work as parents. I call this the "mother as emotional expert" category. In five households neither the husband nor the wife was described by self or other as highly emotional nor as more intuitively connected to the children. In these "shared emotion families" the work of managing emotions was shared. In four families both husband and wife were highly sensitive to emotional nuances, and they seemed to do the emotion work, particularly as parents, intensely. These families had twice the emotional intensity of the others, and I call them "parallel emotion work" families.

Mother as Emotional Expert

In mother-as-emotional-expert families the woman tends to pay more attention to the quality of the marital relationship. She is seen by both partners as more intimately and emotionally connected to the children. In some cases biological essentialist beliefs slip into ideological explanations for why a mother has stronger emotional bonds to the children. Thus, Mr. Potadman explained his wife's greater emotional connection to his sons when they were young by her pregnancy and breast-feeding. His wife explains her closeness this way: "I'm more the family organizer. . . . I'm sort of the schedule person, . . . I'm just by nature more prone to do it, so, you know, I do it. . . . Isaac's a little more of a procrastinator. . . . You know, I probably do more of the emotional kinds of stuff. I mean . . . when somebody's unhappy or stuff like that I go and try to talk to him and try to be available."

In most families the parents simply credit the differences to personality. Ms. Pretzman complained that the one problem in her relationship with her husband was that he did not have a wide range of emotions and was not physically demonstrative. She wished for more intensity in the relationship—more highs and lows. "You can't fight with someone who won't get mad," she complained. The lack of intensity led Ms. Pretzman to look for emotional connection elsewhere, a pattern atypical in fair marriages. She explained, "I don't think he can provide me with the kind of closeness I can get in other friends." Yet there was no indication that Ms. Pretzman was closer emotionally to the children than her husband was.

Rather, each parent claimed to have the closest attachment to the child most like himself or herself.

Finally, the Reluxes both believe that the mother is the more sensitive, emotionally tuned-in partner. Mr. Relux explains how his relationship with the children differs from his wife's: she "pays attention more . . . , she's more sympathetic." Ms. Relux sums up the subjective experience of these families with traditional emotional relationships in her answer to a question about who was more emotionally attached to their daughter in her first year of life: "I think we were both emotionally connected. I would assume that I was more because I'm the mother. . . . She was the most important thing in my life. . . . Everything else just seemed inconsequential."

Interestingly, these men "mothered" their children in every observable or measurable sense—they spent as much time and energy "mothering" as their wives did. Yet they did not mother with such intense emotional connection as their wives did. Their gendered selves were not transformed by their everyday nurturing experiences. The nine men in the other families were quite another story.

Shared Emotion Workers

The five fathers in the shared emotion workers category described themselves and were described by their wives as equal partners in paying attention to the emotional quality of their marital relationships, and they were also intensely connected to their children. What is interesting, however, is that none of the women in this type of family described herself as tightly emotionally bound to her children, as did most of the mothers in the mother-as-emotional-expert group. These couples seemed to sense what an average amount of attention to emotional issues would be and then split the work. The father is as likely to be the worrier or scheduler as the mother, and the mother is as likely to be the disciplinarian as the father. In most such families both parents believe that their children were equally connected to mother and father from earliest infancy. The mothers were not more likely than the fathers to experience pain at separation from their infants when returning to paid work. These parents tended to provide idiosyncratic explanations for the closeness of the relationship of one or the other with a particular child.

In the Oakley family, both parents agree that they are equally connected to both children but that the father was more "emotionally attuned" to the oldest child when he was an infant. "James could get him to go to sleep on his shoulder; I couldn't. Stuff like that. I had to nurse him to get him to go to sleep. James could walk him around. James had actually a lot of experience with kids. His younger brother is thirteen years younger than he is, and he took care of him." In this family the parents can trace how emotional connectedness has changed over time and because of circumstances. In another "shared emotion work" family a mother put it this way: we both just "love her to death," and that seemed to us to be an equal opportunity statement.

Parallel Emotion Workers

In the four families in which both parents are self-consciously and intensively emotionally sensitive there seems to be a doubling of emotion work: a household unusually charged with warmth, and sometimes with jealousy. In one such home the couple consistently use terms of endearment when speaking about or to their spouse. In another family the husband cannot seem to stay away from his wife while she does the dishes, so he rubs her back as she works, singing her little love rhymes. In three of the four families the men are strikingly gentle: one was a conscientious objector to the Vietnam War, another was abused as a child and had been uncomfortable in macho settings as long as he could remember, and another is a vegetarian philosophically opposed to all killing, even of bugs that appear inside his home. These three men simply move gently; even their body language speaks of care and empathy. But the fourth man in this group is tall and athletic: the one conflict in this marriage concerns the amount of time that it is appropriate for him to spend in team sports.

These parallel emotion workers seem to have intense relationships with each other and their children. In these families the parents double their effort rather than split the emotion work. They spend a great deal of time and energy discussing emotions and showering attention on the children. This creates a palpable emotional intensity. The Sykeses, both of whom changed occupations to ones better suited to family life, seem to be a model family. The parents have closer relationships with each other than with anyone else in the world. They rain loving attention on their nine-year-old. The night I observed this home the daughter's bedtime ritual started as her mother spent twenty minutes brushing the child's hair, which reaches to her thighs. Both parents then read her a story about the civil rights movement, using different voices for each character. They discussed questions that arose from the story, such as how it must have felt to be a slave. When the reading was over and the lights went out, the parents squatted on each side of her bed, held her hands, and sang folksongs. In some families bedtime seemed rushed and hectic, but in this home every moment seemed appreciated and precious. While this bedtime scene might have been concocted or at least exaggerated for my benefit, I do not believe that it was. My intuitive feelings, the family's interview responses, and the daughter's blasé response to the routine led me to believe that this was a nightly ritual.

There also, however, seemed to be a negative consequence to such intensive focus on nurturing. Even in this family, in which the father reported "falling head over heels in love" when his baby was born, Mr. Sykes sensed that his daughter was moving from an equal attachment to both parents to a stronger attachment to her mother. This clearly pained him. She has a "growing strengthening of her female identification," he told me. He felt that his daughter's relationship with her mother was "deepening in ways it isn't with me."

A sense of pain when children choose one parent over the other was expressed only in such parallel emotion work families. The wife in the Cross family told us that her older daughter had quickly established herself as a daddy's girl. The father mentioned that this had bothered his wife until their second child was born and reversed the pattern: "Cary was a bit put back at how much Evelyn went for me over her. . . . But Cary got her wish, . . . and that's called Nancy. We each got a child."

The wife's interview confirmed that she had felt rejected but feels better now because she believes that Evelyn is turning back to her mother for heart-to-heart talks and for cuddling. Ms. Cross is not sure, though, and qualifies her answer with a wistful "or maybe that is my desire." Mr. Cross believes that the older daughter is still closer to him, but he admits, sadly, that things seem to be changing. "She's unfortunately old enough to see some of these girls versus boys things, and so she has girl talks with her mom now. I'm losing out."

This sadness at losing out becomes jealousy in some parallel emotion work families. When we asked the Valts how they would feel if one parent decided to quit paid work and stay at home full-time with the children, both parents immediately responded, in separate and independent interviews, "jealous." Ms. Valt explained: "I would be terribly jealous. I would have a problem with it because I would be worried they would love him more and he would have the edge." This competition for children's affection was unexpected; Ms. Valt realized, in retrospect, that she had expected — simply because she was the mother — to retain emotional centrality in her children's hearts. She had assumed that "we'd do as much work, but the kid would still love me a little bit more." She had found that sharing the work equally resulted in sharing the child's deepest affections equally, and this was harder to accept than she had anticipated.

Overall, there was no simple pattern to how these families handled emotions, the cathexis component of their lives.[4] Six of the families showed traditional, gendered patterns of emotional life, with more sensitive wives and mothers and emotionally reserved men. Gendered selves clearly can resist change even when institutional and interactional expectations have changed, even when behavior itself is no longer gender-typed. In most of these families, however, we find parents without fully traditional gendered selves. In four of the families the wives and husbands seemed to have moved to a center—the women seemed less emotionally intense and focused than did traditional wives and mothers, and the men were more emotionally attuned to relationships, often consciously rejecting a macho version of masculinity. In five other families the women seemed as emotionally focused as traditional women, but their husbands were equally focused. Without longitudinal data it is impossible to explain the factors that shaped these different emotional types, but one finding is clear: there is a great diversity in emotional management among our "fair" families.

4. While we have much information on the division of labor in traditional families, little comparative information exists on how these components of cathexis are handled in traditional couples. Surely there are some emotionally distant mothers and doting dads in traditional families. In fact, Russell (1983) finds that even within families who follow a traditional gendered division of labor there are several kinds of fathers: those uninterested and unavailable both emotionally and physically, those available as occasional playmates but not responsible for child care, and "good" fathers who help out their wives both emotionally and physically.

Conclusion

These are couples who have, to a great extent, managed to overcome the gendered structure at the institutional, interactional, and individual levels of analysis. The wives have challenged and overcome many of the disadvantages that women face in the work force; they are well-paid professionals, equal to their husbands in social and economic status. The consequences of the gender structure at the interactional level of analysis are similarly muted, though not entirely absent. The couples have challenged and overcome most of the gendered expectations at the interactional level of analysis. Neither spouse believes that one or the other is or should be solely responsible for earning a living or care for the children. Cognitive images that link sex category and family roles are largely replaced here with a gender-neutral set of expectations. The picture is less consistent at the individual level of analysis. Many of these husbands and wives have begun to transform traditionally gendered aspects of their personalities. Most of the women are forthright, assertive, and task-oriented. None of the wives are quiet, passive, or dependent, and none use their domestic skills to help define them as real women or to do gender. Most of the husbands have similarly challenged traditional models of masculinity. They have adopted ideological commitments to equality and begun to invent a version of masculinity that integrates strength, warmth, and nurturance. They have rejected the hegemonic masculinity embodied by John Wayne; they do not believe that real men must be tough, dominating, competitive, or macho.

What allows these couples to construct fair marriages? There is no one factor. The women are strong and successful, but so are many other career women who are struggling in second-shift marriages or are divorced from men who are not interested in equality. One factor that clearly differentiates these couples from most others is their joint commitment to equality and their challenge to the interactional gendered expectations usually built into heterosexual marriage. They have rejected normative definitions of women's domesticity and men's providership, and they expect equality from each other. Finally, most of the women and men have rejected traditional gendered selves. The women are assertive and ambitious, as well as nurturant and sensitive. But, once again, so are many feminist women whose marriages are not this fair. It is perhaps the men who are most atypical here, who are secure enough to challenge the patriarchal version of masculinity that permeates our culture. They are creating a version of masculinity with an umbrella large enough to cover competition at work and concern with material success, along with domesticity, emotional supportiveness, and nurturance. The transformation of the men in this sample, at the individual level of gendered selves, makes changes at the interactional level of possible.

If the couples introduced in this chapter can teach us anything about the bases on which peer marriages are built, it is that change must occur simultaneously at all levels of the gender structure: women must overcome barriers at the institutional level so that they are not economically dependent subordinant partners; families must redefine domesticity and breadwinning as the responsibility of both parents; and men must replace a hegemonic domineering masculinity with a version of masculinity that includes nurturance and emotional sensitivity. Whether these men and women know it or not (and most, but not all, are conscious of the feminist politics involved), they are in the business of recreating our social structure. They may not be totally post-gendered families, but they are as close as we can imagine toward the turn of the century.

6

Ideology, Experience, Identity

The Complex Worlds of Children in Fair Families

I n this chapter I follow what happens when marital partners committed to fairness become parents. In these households there are few interactional expectations attached to gender. But children grow up not only in their families but also in their schools and with their friends. In this chapter I explore what happens when gendered expectations are changed within the family but not outside of it. What are the consequences for the children's gendered identities, and for their social lives?[1]

There has been no previous research, to my knowledge, on how and whether children raised in egalitarian households differ from those in more traditional families. We found two patterns: the children faced serious inconsistencies between their egalitarian beliefs and their experiences with peers, and their identities seem to be forged more from lived experiences than from ideology (see Risman and Myers 1997 for an earlier discussion of these findings). The disjunction between ideology, experience, and identity seems to be common to all these children's stories. I cannot conclusively show that the patterns identified here are not true for all upper-middle-class white children in contemporary America, but I do not believe that they are. First, as a parent, I have direct access to my daughter's

1. An earlier report of these data about children in fair families is available in Risman and Myers (1997).

friends and to their families, and I rarely see any evidence that most of those children deal with the same issues as those salient to children in these fair families. Second, I can compare these children's experiences to some new gender research on children and make some educated guesses about what makes these children different.

Previous Literature: Developing Gendered Identities

Sociologists have only rarely—and quite recently—studied children's gender. Most of the literature that needs to be reviewed originates in other disciplines. When children are studied in both sociology and psychology, the predominant questions center on how children learn to be boys or girls. That is, most of the past literature falls squarely into the individualist level of analysis—seeking to explain how male and female babies develop into gendered boys and girls. This individualist literature on children can be organized analytically by presumptions about children's role in their own socialization. I divide this scholarship into three categories: that which sees children as the primary *actors* in the gendering process; that which sees children's gender as something *imposed* by the larger culture and reinforced by rewards and punishments; and that which argues that children are constrained by longstanding gender norms but which sees children as *participating in and negotiating* the enactment of gender.

Self-Gendering

Theories of cognitive development have addressed children's role in learning gendered expectations. Piaget (1932) and Kohlberg (1966) argued that children play an active role in gender acquisition. Children do not passively absorb information from their parents and peers but seek relevant information, and they organize it into predictable patterns. They begin to do this at a young age in order to make sense of their worlds. According to Kohlberg, children choose gender as a major organizing principle because it jibes with their desire for order. Children come to view gender as "natural" differences between males and females. Piaget and other cognitive development theorists argue that children see same-sex modeling as morally necessary and invariant (Kohlberg 1966; Maccoby 1992; Martin 1993). This perspective puts undue emphasis on the child as a rational actor who freely selects gender from the available options. There is a chicken-and-egg conundrum here. Children are born into the existing social structure and are affected accordingly; they do not randomly reproduce gender. Writers in this perspective have tended to presume that gender dichotomies are not only salient but necessary for the psychological development of children. Thus, while children are seen as actors, this perspective ignores the power of gender stratification on children's cognitive processes. Still, one could imagine that children raised in a family without gender dichotomies might self-gender less systematically.

Socialization Imposed on Passive Recipients

Scholars at the other end of the spectrum have often focused on how the existing gender order constrains the socialization of children. Beginning with Parsons and Bales (1955) and Inkeles (1968), scholars in this tradition see socialization as a one-way conduit of information from adult to child. In particular, parents and other adults apply to children stereotypes of behavior based on the child's sex. This typing begins at birth (Deaux 1984; Fagot, Leinbach, and C. O'Boyle 1992; Hutson 1983; Stern and Karraker 1989). Bandura (1962, 1971) argues that parents, teachers, and peers all reward children for learning the behavior of the same sex. Because they receive positive feedback for "correct" behavior, children imitate same-sex behavior and "encode" it into their behavioral repertoires. Once encoded, the child's gender is set.

Scholars of sex roles assert that the gendering of children is complete at an early age. The acquisition of appropriate gender characteristics and expectations is not optional for the child. The important impact of scholarship on gender socialization is the realization that, because we treat boys and girls differently, they develop different skills and desires (Renzetti and Curan 1992; Richardson 1981). In this view, different treatment helps to create people who *are* socially different. By imposing different constraints and expectations society helps to create a self-fulfilling prophesy that perpetuates gender inequality. However, the socialization perspective of gender learning offers a static picture of gender, with the child as a relatively acquiescent recipient of appropriate models of behavior that in turn offer little room for improvisation and change (Kreps et al. 1994). Within this perspective one would logically argue that children rewarded for gender-atypical behavior would develop less gender-typed personalities and identities.

Acting, Not Just Reacting

Sociologists have begun to argue that gender socialization of children is more than just adults providing role models and sanctions, with children hitting, missing, and eventually getting it "right" (Corsaro 1985; Alanen 1988). Instead, they are finding that children actually participate in the process. This emerging tradition integrates a concern with the development of gendered selves via cognitive schemas with attention to the power of interactional expectations. Children are influenced not only by the adult world (self-gendering and socialization) but also by each other. For example, Borman and O'Reilly (1987) find that kindergarteners in same-sex play groups initiate play in similar ways but that the topics for play vary by gender. That is, boys and girls play different types of games, creating different conversational and negotiation demands. Thorne (1993) observed groups of children in classrooms and school yards, noting how they create and police gender boundaries and form various strata among themselves. She asserts that gender relations are not invariant but can change according to the context and the actors involved. Thorne has criticized most socialization and development frameworks because they presuppose a certain outcome: that boys will learn appropriate masculinities, girls will learn appropriate femininities; and if they fail to do so they will either be punished or relegated to the ranks of deviants. She argues that such a future-oriented perspective distorts children's everyday realities, which are crucial to their ongoing gendered negotiations. "Children's interactions are not preparation for life," she writes. "They are life itself" (3).

Bem (1993) similarly improves on both cognitive and socialization theories by linking them. She argues that children try to make sense of the world by forming categories, or schemas, but says that these categories are shaped by existing gender categories in society. Gender is subtly transmitted to children by adults both consciously and unconsciously, so that the dominant way of understanding the social world is usually seen as the best way to understand it. Existing gender divisions are nearly hegemonic and often unquestioned by both children and adults. Therefore, questioning the taken-for-granted gendered organization of society is difficult and unlikely.

It seems reasonable that all three processes occur. Children who live in gendered societies no doubt develop gender schemas and will code themselves, as well as the world around them, in gendered terms. But this seems much more likely to be the result of their lived experiences in patriarchal societies than the consequence of an innate drive for cognitive development. While children are developing cognitive gender schemas, adults and older children are treating boys and girls quite differently. Gender socialization is apparent in any observation of children's lives. And while children are being socialized they react to, negotiate, and even reject some societal pressures. Although children are actors in the gendering process, we must not ignore the impact of differential reinforcement of gender-appropriate behavior. The cognitive effects of living in a gendered (and sexist) society, the reality of gender socialization, and the active efforts of boys and girls to negotiate their own worlds interact to shape their daily lives, and perhaps to affect their future options.

Unequal Outcomes: Reproducing Gender Difference and Inequality

Even when we recognize that children are both actors and reactors in the gendering process, we cannot overlook the strong empirical data which suggest that most boys and girls are differentially prepared for adulthood. Boys are still routinely socialized to learn to work in teams and to compete, and girls are still routinely socialized to value nurturing (note the relative numbers of boys and girls in team sports versus those dedicated to the popular Babysitters Club book series). Thorne (1993) has shown convincingly that there is much more crossover gender play than dichotomous thinking presumes, yet other research continues to indicate the consequences of gender socialization on children (Lever 1978; Luttrell 1993; Hawkins 1985; Wilder, Mackie, and Cooper 1985; Signorelli 1990; Maccoby 1992; Hutson 1983). There is also much evidence that gender socialization differs by social class, ethnicity, and religion (Peterson and Rollins 1987; Collins 1990).

Socialization clearly happens both in children's play and in their families. Lever's (1978) classic study of boys' and girls' play offers insight into how boys and girls are prepared for a future in which men are presumed to belong in the public, competitive sphere and women in the private, nurturing sphere. Boys' games were more likely to be outside, involve teams, and be age-integrated. Girls were more likely to play make-believe games with one or two others and to break up a game rather than work through conflict. These differences are well developed by the middle of elementary school. Parents and immediate family are also obviously an important source of transmission for gendered expectations (Maccoby 1992). Research indicates that parents participate in gender-typing by often rewarding gender-typical play and punishing gender-atypical play (Bem 1993; Hutson 1983).

While several scholars have documented that some families are moving toward shared parenting and more liberal gender socialization for children, we have little information about how effective such changes in parenting style might be in a society in which gendering processes continue to occur (Coltrane 1996; Schwartz 1994; Segal 1990). It is to this question of how children in egalitarian families fare that I now turn our attention.

Children in Fair Families

The parents of the children discussed here have attempted to break the chain of gender inequality that typically begins at birth. These children are living in a context different from that in more mainstream families: most of these parents make a conscious effort *not* to replicate what Connell (1987) calls hegemonic masculinities and emphasized femininities. They have an ideological and practical commitment to organizing their homes and families in an egalitarian manner. Whereas mainstream parents may react with delight when their daughter wants to be Barbie for Halloween and their son wants toy guns for his birthday, these parents are likely to be dismayed. Their children are growing up in a world where gender does not dictate who does what or who has more power, at least not in the family. Rather than receiving reinforcement from their parents when they enact hegemonic behavior, these children are likely to encounter disappointment or concern. So how do these children negotiate gender, given their atypical parents?

To understand these children's perspectives on their own lives we had to create cognitively appropriate research instruments. After six months of planning we decided on three separate formats for the children: an interview schedule with questions resembling stories for the four- through six-year-olds; an interview format that included some questions, some writing of poems, and some free play for seven- through ten-year-olds; and interviews that included open-ended questions and some paper-and-pencil items for the older children. There were twenty-six children in these fifteen families, but five were under four years of age, too young to interview. We interviewed twelve boys and nine girls. Ten of the children were between four and six, seven children were between seven and ten, and four children were at least eleven. Three of the four older children were from the same family, so I refrain from making any generalizations about that group.

These children live in complex worlds. They must navigate complicated social and cognitive landscapes. Three themes emerged from our conversations and observations. First, the parents seem to be very successful at transferring their ideological values to their children. The youngsters believe that men and women are equal, or ought to be. Second, these children's experiences at school and with their peers have taught them unequivocally that boys and girls are not similar, nor do they think they should be. Boys and girls are—in these children's minds—totally different kinds of people. Third, identities seem more forged from experiences with peers than from ideology. The boys in particular seem to struggle to reconcile their identities and their beliefs.

Ideology

Sixteen of the twenty-one children we interviewed had entirely adopted their parents' egalitarian or feminist views on gender, and two of the children without such views were four-year-olds whose answers were better described as inconsistent than traditional. The children know that occupations are currently sex-segregated but believe they should not be. They do not see any tasks in families that ought to be exclusively for either men or women. One nine-year-old boy actually became annoyed at the line of questioning about what men and women should do. He rolled his eyes and retorted, "I told you I think anybody can do these jobs. . . . I think that saying just men or just women could do these jobs isn't being equal." In contrast, most four-year-olds assign sex-stereotypic labels to activities, occupations, and playthings (Bornstein and Lamb 1988).

Most of the children, both boys and girls, not only believe that men and women should be free to work in any occupation and should share the family labor, but also understand that male privilege exists in contemporary society. A nine-year-old girl told us that she believes very much in feminism because "I don't think that it is the least bit fair that in most places males have the main power. I think that women play an important part and should be free to do what they want to do." Similarly, a fifteen-year-old told us, in response to a question about what he likes about being a boy, "It's probably easier being a guy. At least it is now because of stereotypes and prejudices and everything." Overall, most of these children were sophisticated true believers in the capabilities of men and women to perform the same jobs and family roles. The influence of their parents as ideological conduits and role models is evident in their attitudes.

Experiences

These children may have liberal attitudes about gender equality for men and women, but when that ideology contradicts their experiences as boys and girls, life wins hands down. Despite their post-gender answers to what is appropriate for adults, these children give stereotypical answers about the differences between boys and girls. In order to find out their gut beliefs about boys and girls we probed their experiences with a variety of techniques. We asked how their lives would be different if a magician turned them into the opposite sex. We provided short scenarios using stereotypically male and female adjectives (e.g., weak, strong, fearful, adventuresome) and asked them to tell us which adjectives described girls and which described boys and why. We asked what they liked and disliked about being a girl or boy. We asked them to write poems beginning with the line "If I were a boy/girl" using the opposite sex category. We showed them pictures of a boy and a girl, sitting side by side on a sofa, and asked them to tell us a story about each child. We followed up every comment that would help us assess their attitudes.

Although none of the four- to six-year-olds have begun to believe that boys and girls are different, most children from mainstream families clearly have strong gender schemas by this age (Bem 1993). Their egalitarian parents have managed to insulate the preschoolers from typical American norms, perhaps by their choice of paid caregiving arrangements and friends. Once the children reached seven years of age, however, their nonfamilial experiences broadened considerably, as did their ideas about differences between the sexes. We find the descriptions of school-age children remarkably consistent and stereotypical across sex and age categories. Girls are sweet and neat; boys are athletic and disruptive. And these descriptions are consistent with those given by children, presumably from more mainstream families, in other research (Bornstein and Lamb 1988). Table 6.1 contains adjectives used in direct quotes about boys. The age and sex of the speakers who use each adjective at least once are indicated. Of the sixteen adjectives used, half describe socially disruptive personality traits, often considered aspects of masculinity.

Table 6.1. Adjectives Used to Describe Boys

Adjective	Speakers by gender and age			
Active	7-year-old girl			
Into sports	7-year-old girl	12-year-old boy	10-year-old boy	9-year-old girl
Mean	7-year-old girl	15-year-old boy	4-year-old girl	
Bad	7-year-old girl	9-year-old girl		
More free	11-year-old girl			
Sarcastic	15-year-old boy			
Cool	4-year-old girl			
Aggressive	12-year-old boy	10-year-old boy	9-year-old girl	
Athletic	12-year-old boy	10-year-old boy		
Tough	12-year-old boy			
Stronger	6-year-old boy	10-year-old boy		
Into fighting	10-year-old boy	9-year-old girl		
Troublemaking	10-year-old boy	9-year-old girl		
Competitive	9-year-old girl			
Bully	10-year-old boy			
Into computers	4-year-old boy			

Table 6.2. Adjectives Used to Describe Girls

Adjective	Speakers by gender and age		
Nice	10-year-old boy	4-year-old girl	12-year-old boy
Well-behaved	10-year-old boy	7-year-old girl	
Quiet	10-year-old boy	10-year-old boy	7-year-old girl
Cooperative	9-year-old girl		
Good	9-year-old girl		
Sweet	7-year-old girl		
Not into sports	10-year-old boy		
Not sneaky	12-year-old boy		
Nicer to friends	12-year-old boy		
Less free	11-year-old girl		

The rest are more neutral descriptors but are still stereotypically male. The world that these school-age children know is one in which boys as a group are athletic and mean.

We elicited more comments about boys than about girls—girls are described almost as a second species. But again the comments were remarkably consistent. All of the adjectives describe traditional feminine stereotypes (table 6.2). Six of the adjectives are socially valued personality traits, the others more neutral. The children voiced unequivocal belief in major sex differences between boys and girls just minutes after parroting their parents' feminist views about the equality and similarity of men and women.

Three of these children did qualify their stereotypical answers. One eight-year-old boy made a point of telling us that he knew that girls could be into sports or computers, he just did not know any who were. A seven-year-old girl was sure that girls were better behaved and that boys were mean, but she also sometimes wanted to be a boy because they seemed to have more playful and active games. A ten-year-old boy knew that some girls were "like boys," and he was even letting such a girl try out for his spy club. And one five-year-old boy made the acute observation that girls played different games than boys did when at school on the playground, but when in the neighborhood they played the same games together.

When family experiences collided with experiences with peers, the family influences were dwarfed. For example, a six-year-old boy told us that if a magician were to turn him into a girl, he'd be different because he would have long hair. This boy's father had a ponytail that reached the middle of his back, and the mother's hair was hardly below her ears. A four-year-old boy told us that if a magician were to turn him into a girl, he'd have to do housework—this from the son of a father whose flexible work schedule has allowed him to spend more time in domestic pursuits than his wife does.

It almost seems as if these children believe that boys and girls are opposites but that men and women are magically transformed into equal and comparable people. The children know that men and women are equal; it is boys and girls who are totally different.

Seven of these children spoke explicitly about male privilege among peers or at school. An eleven-year-old girl told us that sometimes she wished to be a boy because when

> teachers need help like to carry a box to their classroom, they always come in and say, like, "Can I borrow a couple of your boys," and never say, "Can I borrow a couple of your students?" And so the girls never get to do any of the stuff and leave the classroom. . . . It's always the boys that get to leave. And, like, little trips and stuff, when we used to go on field trips, the boys would always have to carry a basket of lunches and go ahead, and when

they had stuff to bring from the car, it'd always be
boys that would get to go to the car. . . . The girls,
like, had to stay on the bus and just sit there and
wait while some boys got to go there and the girls
never got to do it, do that stuff . . . You get left out
because you're a girl. . . . But I'm not wimpy.

A seven-year-old girl told us that she was "more hyper" than most
girls and that many of her friends were boys because they were
more active and playful. A ten-year-old boy mentioned "racism
against women" in sports. A nine year-old-girl was an avowed feminist with implicit essentialist notions about girls' innate coopera-
tiveness versus boys' innate combativeness. She thought girls ought
to have more power in the world because they were better people.

This is the response an eight-year-old boy gave to us when he
was asked to write a poem about what it would be like to be a
girl. His understanding of male privilege was widely shared if not
usually so well articulated.

If I were a girl I'd have to attract a guy
wear makeup; sometimes.
Wear the latest style of clothes and try to be likable.
I probably wouldn't play any physical sports like football or soccer.
I don't think I would enjoy myself around men
in fear of rejection
or under the pressure of attracting them.

While both boys and girls "knew" that boys were troublemakers,
sarcastic, and athletic, this boy also saw clearly that girls had major
disadvantages.

Only a few of the boys were aware that they belonged to a group
for which they had internalized negative characteristics. One such
boy answered our question about how he was different from other

guys this way: "I think I'm taller. I don't like bullying people around that much. . . . When one of my friends starts fighting somebody or arguing with somebody I don't join in. I steer clear of them. I try to get in as few fights as possible." This boy built his identity on sports (his room was a baseball shrine, and his activities were sports, sports, and more sports) but tried to distance himself from the violent aspects of peer group masculinity. Another boy told us that if he were transformed into a girl he would be nicer to his friends. These boys had internalized negative attitudes toward their own group and, at some level, themselves. In no case did any girl tell us how bad girls were as a group. When girls talked about how they were similar to and different from other girls, their answers were idiosyncratic (e.g., taller or shorter, longer hair, better reader). These children "know" that boys and girls are different, they "know" that boys have advantages, but they also "know" that girls are nicer people.

Identity

These children are very consistent when they explain how boys and girls are different. The unanimity dissolves when we begin to look at how they are forging their own identities. Only six of the children seem to have fashioned selves that unambiguously fit their own stereotyped notions about childhood gender. The interview and observational data collected in these families identify six children who describe themselves in consistently gendered fashion and were so identified in observational data.

The first obvious finding is that these children's attitudes and identities are not necessarily correlated. Of the six children with stereotypical gendered selves, one boy and three girls are also self-consciously egalitarian, even feminist. The two other children in this category had more traditional beliefs about gender.

As the tables above show, the children suggested that boys were active, into sports, mean, bad, freer than girls, sarcastic, cool, aggressive, athletic, tough, stronger than girls, into fights, troublemakers, competitive, bullies, and into computers. I use the label "all-boy" boys and "all-girl" girls to describe children who portray characteristics exclusively in one of the two tables. No child manifested every characteristic on our list, but the two children in the all-boy category and the four girls in the all-girl group could not be described with any of the adjectives on the opposite-sex list. For example, there was no indication that the Pretzman boy was mean or a troublemaker—just the opposite. He followed our directions closely and appeared to be very sweet. Yet all his interests were stereotypically masculine—sports, Legos, *Star Trek,* computers. He described himself as "strong" and used that criterion to differentiate boys and girls. He didn't play much with girls, and there was no indication of cross-gender behavior or traits either in the interview or as we watched him at home. The twelve-year-old Potadman boy was similar. His main interest and identity seemed to be attached to sports. He answered us with short, not-too-reflective comments. In traditionally masculine fashion, he described his friendships almost entirely in terms of sharing activities.

I categorize the four girls as all-girl because they can be described using the characteristics the children provided for us about girls: nice, well-behaved, quiet, cooperative, good, sweet, not into sports, not sneaky, nice to friends. None of these girls embodied every one of these traits, but it is unlikely that they would be described by any of the traits on the other list. One shared characteristic was their distaste for competitive sports. The eleven-year-old Germane girl provides an easy comparison with the twelve-year-old Potadman boy. Her favorite games were fantasies, her favorite activity was dance, her favorite possessions were dolls and stuffed animals. The Stokes ten-year-old was similarly gendered. Her favorite activities were reading, writing poems, and art. She is adamant about disliking sports, and she knows why: she doesn't like any activity where you have to be pushy or aggressive. The six-year-old Green daughter had three dollhouses, and there was not a "boy" toy in the house. Her parents were very conscious of encouraging her to make her own choices and to develop her own potential; the mother told us she was trying to get her daughter to be willing to play some sports, at least at school during recess.

These six children, raised by egalitarian parents and often holding feminist attitudes themselves, have nevertheless fashioned selves that are unambiguously gendered. The following poem sums up what these children think about even imagining being the opposite sex. The poem was written by the Sykes girl in response to our request to write a verse that begins "If I were a boy": "If I were a boy, I'd know my parents had made a mistake and that I should have been a girl. I'd always feel that I didn't belong because the girls were who I wanted to play with but they wouldn't let me, and I didn't want to be with the boys."

This nine-year-old provides an interesting example of the disjunction between identity and ideology. She lives in one of the most self-consciously feminist and progressive families in our study. They see themselves as outside the mainstream. They have no television set so that their daughter will avoid excess materialism. Both parents and daughter are avowed feminists. The daughter is one of the most feminine in the sample—her long wavy hair flows below her waist. She collects china teacups, hates competitive sports, and loves nature and hiking. She saved a bug from death during my home observation and carried it tenderly outside. In my honor she put on her favorite nightgown, ankle-length and with a pink bow. This child is very smart, and she intends to succeed professionally, maybe in a scientific career. So despite her feminine self-presentation and dislike for most things male, she actually crosses gender boundaries in other ways.

The other fifteen children have also fashioned gendered selves. The boys are much more likely to like sports, the girls to like dance. Despite their parents' role-modeling, despite their own ideology, all these girls are more feminine than masculine and all these boys are more masculine than feminine. But the rest of the children, to varying degrees, cross gender lines in interests and interpersonal style. All but one of the girls is either involved in at least one competitive sport or expects to be when she is a little older. All the boys stand out in some way as exceptions to hegemonic masculinity. An interesting sex difference exists, however. All the girls told us in quite explicit terms just how they were different from other girls, but the boys often denied any differences from other boys—differences that our interview and observational team noted. For example, the Cody daughter knows that she is different from other girls because she loves team sports, and she would like to be a boy except that she knows "they aren't always very nice." A four-year-old girl likes to climb trees as well as play fantasy games about babies. She knows she is "nice, like other girls," but she wants to be "cool," like boys. She told us her future goal was to "be a mommy so I can work hard and like my job." The Cross girl believes that she is more active than other girls, but she is also "real sweet," likes horses, and is nice to her friends (all characteristics that she says make her different from boys). The Relux six-year-old told us that she is "not like other girls particularly." She has friends who are boys, although her best friend is another girl. But she likes being a girl because she can do whatever she wants.

The boys coded as portraying some crossover behaviors and interpersonal style were much less likely than the girls to notice it themselves. Although some of the data reported here come directly from the interviews, this analysis also relies on subtle inconsistencies in their own words, body language, and to some extent intuition of the part of the interview and observational team, as recorded in field notes. The older Potadman boys (fifteen and seven-teen years of age) told us of some hopes and dreams that seemed to cross gender stereotypes. The fifteen-year-old babysits and loves to vacuum and cook. He would like to stay home with his children if his wife could earn a high enough income. His very tall older brother, whose ponytail reaches below his waist, hates to work out and finds it unfair that women can be considered sexy without being muscular but that men cannot. He writes poetry and never has been much into sports, though he does like volleyball. He de-scribes himself as an intellectual outsider and seems comfortable—if somewhat vulnerable—with the status.

Four little boys also reported androgynous preferences. The four-year-old Cody boy likes many boys' games, particularly base-ball. But he also wants to be like his sister, plays housekeeping at day care, and enjoys playing dress-up in his sister's clothes. The four-year-old Trexler son has favorite movie characters: Aladdin and the Little Mermaid. The four-year-old Relux boy thinks that being "silly" is the best part of being a boy. While he likes guns and has mostly boys as friends, his answers to most questions seem gender-neutral. Similarly, the five-year-old Cary boy likes boys' toys and baseball, but many of his favorite activities seem to be gender-neutral, such as board games and playing outside with both boys and girls. His body language and self-presentation led to the de-scription of him as "gentle" in the field notes. The six-year-old Staton son prefers stereotypically boys' toys, and he takes tai kwon do lessons, but, like the fifteen-year-old Potadman boy, he would like to not work at all so that he could "spend more time with his kids." These boys never seemed rough or tough; even when talking about their stereotypical behaviors they seemed warm and caring.

There were two boys whose words contradicted their behavior (as reported by their parents) and our observations. The ten-year-old Oakley boy seemed to try too hard at his self-presentation. He wanted us to think he was tough, mean, and sneaky, a "real" boy. But the boy we met was warm, kind, and soft-spoken, even as he told us about his war games. This son of two writers wanted a blue-collar job for which he could wear "lots of armor" and be tough. But these words didn't square with what we saw: a ten-year-old who played gently with his four-year-old sister. He interrupted his own and his sister's interview to take her to look out the bathroom window so that she did not miss the full moon. They fought during our home interview, and he hurt her by mistake. He was genuinely sorry, offering his "butt" for her to hit in response. When we noticed some Barbie dolls in his closet and asked what kind of games he played with them, he answered, "Oh, I mostly kill them in war games. They're my sisters." But his mother told us that both children played fantasy games with the dolls. He alluded to this himself later: "I like the Ken doll because he is a basketball star." This boy twitched when he spoke about gender preferences. I found the interview poignant: he knew that boys were supposed to be mean and sneaky, and he wanted very much to fulfill those expectations, or at least to make us believe that he did. But we couldn't believe it. He was too nice a child.

Another interviewer had a similar experience with the ten-year-old Woods boy. His identity was sports based: he was a baseball fanatic, and his room was entirely in Carolina Blue. He talked about liking to compete. And yet he described his baby brother in loving terms, and in three straight losses in a card game he showed no competitive spirit or disappointment. He emanated warmth, as did his father. He also differentiated himself from other boys because he was not a bully and did not like to fight.

Conclusion

These data illustrate the usefulness of the theoretical model offered in this book. Although gender structure exists at the institutional, interactional, and individual levels, its consequences are far from predetermined. The children discussed here are being raised in social settings in which gender expectations and interactional demands have been consciously changed to value gender equality. And the children in fair families have adopted their parents' egalitarian views. They say that men and women are equal and that no jobs—inside or outside the family—ought to be sex-typed. But beyond these abstract belief statements these children depend on their own lived experiences for understanding gender. And they "know" that boys and girls are very different.

Boys, as a group, are described—even by boys themselves—as not only athletic but also mean and troublesome. Girls are described as sweet, quiet, and well behaved. And yet it is clear that both boys and girls value, at some level, the masculine over the feminine, or at least the privileges that accompany male status. They notice that boys have more freedom at school and that most boys play harder and with more autonomy. Six of these children met their own criteria for being all boy or all girl; the rest exhibited some cross-gender behavior. The girls knew and reported how they were different from other girls; the boys did not. Gendered selves are changing here, but the change is uneven, with attitudes toward others changing faster than identities. Thorne (1993) shows that children from more mainstream families also cross gender boundaries. Some boys from traditional families also develop soft and gentle selves, and girls from traditional homes can be seen aggressively entering boys' games on the playground. But Thorne gives no indication that children from more traditional families struggle with the inconsistencies among their beliefs, their extrafamilial experiences, and their developing identities.

The parents in fair families are transmitting new cognitive images or gender rules to their children. And though this process is hardly direct or perfectly effective, the children of these families seem to be adopting their parents' gender rules about adult responsibilities. But when it comes to developing their own identities, these children seem to be at least as influenced by the cognitive images and folk knowledge learned from peers as those messages from home. The children struggle with the contradictions between their parentally influenced ideologies and the cognitive images that dominate peer-group culture. In how they fashion their identities, their gendered selves, we can see why social change moves so slowly at the individual level.

Yet, the parents in fair families also were raised in peer cultures with traditional cognitive images about gender and somehow have managed to create new ones for themselves. Their children are the product of a gender structure in flux. Most of them, while clearly developing gendered selves, are also crossing gender boundaries even as they subscribe to the ruling cognitive images in their own culture, which still define boys and girls as opposites. Each time a girl admits that she is not like other girls because she likes sports, each time a little boy differentiates himself from boys as a group because he does not like to fight, the cognitive image begins to blur. Eventually, perhaps, with some adult intervention, those childhood cognitive images might crack and dissolve, to be re-created in a post-gendered society. What is even more clear, however, is that as these children grow into adulthood and move into more egalitarian settings, they are well prepared to reconstruct post-gendered identities. There is no reason to believe that the identities and selves they adopt to negotiate their sexist and gendered childhood worlds will determine the selves they adopt later in life, as their social situations and the expectations they face change.

These data are very clear on another important point, too. These children are growing up to be happy, healthy, and well adjusted in egalitarian, gender-atypical families. They are doing well in families in which both parents are committed to labor force participation and in which fathers are actively nurturing their children. These families dramatically depart from what many fundamentalist Judeo-Christian traditionalists and contemporary political conservatives have argued is the "natural" family—with patriarchal breadwinning fathers and homemaking mothers. Children raised in families with attentive and loving feminist parents do just fine.

But what is also clear is that changing families alone does not allow children to live post-gendered lives. Parents may have the power to change their marriage and their childrearing techniques, but effective social change requires collective action and coalitions across families, schools, and friendship networks. Social change cannot be effective at the level of identities only; it must occur simultaneously at the level of identities, interactions, and institutions.

7

Toward a Dizzy but Liberating Future

n his book *Masculinities,* Connell writes of a utopian future in which gender is deconstructed but avoids the problems of what he labels gender vertigo, the dizziness that we would feel without gendered selves and interactional expectations to give meaning to our lives. In this chapter I argue that Connell is correct, that we must decompose gender, but I also argue that gender vertigo is an intermediate goal, a historical moment that is discomforting but necessary. It holds the exciting possibilities of radically revising our world.

To make this argument I must recap the theoretical theme that I introduced in Chapter 2 and the empirical support for the theory presented elsewhere in this book. I have suggested that we reconceptualize gender as a social structure built into the very fabric of our society, with implications at every level of analysis—for selves, for interaction, and for institutions. Gender is not fixed into our genes, nor is it merely a product of socialized personalities. Gender is, of course, socialized into our personalities, but it also sets the parameters for interactional expectations and is built into our social institutions. I have gone beyond providing this conceptual scheme, however, by suggesting that gendered expectations in American families are major impediments to further movement toward equality. In this chapter I argue that it is indeed possible and necessary to get beyond gendered expectations if we seek to create a just world. Although in a just world all forms of inequality would need to be abolished, I see gender justice as an inextricable aspect of progressive social change. In this book I offer directions for addressing the gendered component of inequality and do not take on the more ambitious but necessary task of proposing change tactics for every aspect of inequality.

My research over the past decade has indicated that even though gender structure is powerful, it is not determinative. Structural determinism is a fallacy. Structures constrain and enable, but they are also human inventions, and as individuals and families develop new ways to live, the gender structure itself evolves. I believe, however, that any gender structure, even one with more room for diversity and more concern for equality than the current one, will inevitably disadvantage women economically and restrict the full humanity of both men and women. I have no direct empirical evidence that a society without any gender structure is possible, for none has ever existed. But the empirical evidence presented here (and by other feminist social scientists over the past two decades) is evidence that a post-gendered future is possible. Gender expectations are socially constructed and sustained by socialization, interactional expectations, and institutional arrangements. When individuals and collectivities change socialization, expectations, and institutions, the gender structure changes. Logically, then, if we no longer use biological sex to differentiate people in their social development or in interpersonal expectations, and if we concurrently degender our institutional arrangements, we could create a world without gender. It is that vision of a post-gendered family in a post-gendered world that I believe to be one goal of liberation.

Gender as a Social Structure

I have argued throughout this book that gender is a social structure that is the basis for sexual stratification. Once such a structure exists—and gender structures are apparent in every known society thus far—it both enables and constrains action, inevitably privileging some people over others and nearly always subordinating women to men. The gender structure organizes action on individual, interactional, and institutional levels. I have further argued that the continuing gender stratification in contemporary American families is better explained by focusing on how the institutional arrangements shape contextual expectations than by relying on how women and men make personal gendered choices.

Gender structure can be conceived at the interactional level of both cultural rules and cognitive images, as tacit knowledge or expectations attached to sex category. Such images are experienced as social facts whether or not the actors deviate from them, as they exist independent of their internalization as personality. The crux of my argument has been that gender rules, as social objects, influence behavior even when the actors involved do not subscribe to them as personal norms. They can be followed or rejected, but in either case they must be attended to. The taken-for-granted acting out of nearly invisible expectations usually re-creates inequality between women and men even when gender per se is irrelevant to the actual task at hand. But rejecting contemporary expectations and negotiating new ways of interacting begins the process of forging new structures. In some of the families whom I studied, the wife-mother's absence forced the father to negotiate a way to "mother" his children. In the feminist families, women's commitment to work or to the couple's egalitarian philosophy led them to reject contemporary male-dominated family structures and pave new paths.

The research discussed in this book provides empirical support for the theory that gender is a social structure with implications at all three levels of analysis, but a structure that can be changed. The single fathers I studied had been raised in an era when men were expected to be family breadwinners, not primary caretakers. Indeed, none of the men had explicitly chosen to "mother" their children, yet they did. When the men's traditional gendered identities collided with the counter-normative expectations to provide primary care for their motherless children, they were able to respond. Indeed, the most interesting finding from the research is that fathers who became primary caretakers because of deceased or deserting wives actually came to think of themselves as having personality traits that are traditionally labeled feminine. The research shows that elements within the gender structure can be overcome—in this case, the expectation that nurturing is women's work—and that when this is done, other consequences of gender as a structure can also be disrupted. Of course, these single men faced the same work-family conflicts that single mothers have always known; there was no change in the structural arrangement of the economy in which workers are presumed to have wives or not to need them. When our attention turned to how women have juggled paid work with family work we saw once again how the contexts faced in adulthood are stronger explanations for life choices than gender socialization, although that does continue to have some implications.

The research on fair families clearly shows that, despite the gendered cultural rules and institutional arrangements, some dual-worker professionals can and are turning their cultural capital (e.g., educational status and career success) into leverage for rejecting the contemporary gender structure. The fifteen families whose lives we shared, if briefly, understand that they are doing things differently. They are raising children with egalitarian gender ideologies, if not gender-free personalities. They have redefined gender expectations as they relate to marriage and parenthood. The husbands and fathers in fair families are pioneering new forms of masculinities. Cognitive gender images, once consciously rejected, are nearly irrelevant to how these husbands and wives organize their most intimate personal relationships as spouses and parents. They have escaped, in large part, the consequences of gendered economic institutions by strategically choosing positions that are flexible enough to allow good parenting.

In today's capitalist economy, only an elite group has the opportunity for such economic choices. Poor, working-class, and even most middle-class families do not have the choices available to privileged, educated professionals. And yet if more and more families demand that our workplaces presume that all paid workers are also family workers, we would see radical changes in the structuring of our economy. Collective action, whether through unionization or political mobilization, can lead to state policy that requires companies to institute family-friendly work rules. The flexible work environments reported by the families in my feminist sample ought to be available to all families.

Together, these research endeavors support my argument that in American families today, it is a combination of interactional and institutional consequences that retard social change, not the gendered personalities, which often are blamed. Individuals are not simply choosing to live gendered lives in traditional nuclear, male-dominated families. Single mothers are not simply choosing to raise children without male partners because that seems easier or more fun; our gendered expectations for men simply do not require or expect them to remain emotionally connected caretakers to children unless they are married to the children's mothers. The cultural images attached to gender and the gendered presumptions built into our institutions are working in tandem to maintain the status quo.

The families about whom I have written in this book are atypical, but the issues they face are ubiquitous. All of us struggle with meeting culturally dictated expectations, defining personal needs, and negotiating the interface between them. Other families whom I might have studied also are challenging the gender structure at the interactional level: single mothers who are both breadwinners and nurturers, gay couples whose parenting styles do not follow gender scripts, or child-free women who choose to forgo motherhood despite its centrality in the cultural definition of womanhood. My goal here has not been to document every gender-atypical intimate relationship. Rather, my goal for discussing these families was to provide empirical evidence that gender can be changed at the level of cognitive images and expectations. Gender structure is contestable. The single fathers and feminist families are success stories; creating a new kind of family is possible even without macrosocietal change. The fair families further show that gender-equitable families can be good places for children.

As women routinely remain paid workers even when married and divorce becomes an even more societally accepted option, family change seems inevitable in the next century. If families are to change in democratic directions, to provide opportunities for human growth and development, we must move beyond organizing family roles around gender itself. The research reported here shows that gender can be changed at the interactional level when institutional or situational changes require it or individuals have the motivation to desire it.

Cracking the Structure

I have tried to show that while gender is a social structure, it is a human invention and thus subject to reinvention and re-creation. In particular, I have focused on how individuals can and do rebel and innovate and begin to change the structure itself.

There are many examples of the ways that institutional change — fostered sometimes by state policies — can encourage gender equality. Flexible working hours, paid parental leave, and part-time career opportunities can make and have made a difference in breaking down gender barriers (Lorber 1994; Coltrane 1996; Gerson 1985, 1993). But the reality remains: most of these policies have had the effect, thus far, of easing women's double burdens. Even in countries like Sweden, where the goal of gender equality is explicit in the legislation, parental leave and part-time work are primarily women's solutions to the struggles of combining paid employment and motherhood (Haas 1992). Such institutional changes, while necessary, can never be sufficient. For the gender structure exists not only on the institutional, individual, and interactional levels, but on all levels at the same time.

This is as far as empirical data can take us. From here, imagining the future demands value-driven creativity. As we enter the twenty-first century I see no way to disentangle gender from inequality, from repressing parts of humanity in women's and men's psyches and identities, from expectations of female subordination in cross-sex interaction, and from institutional arrangements that presuppose workers to be disembodied non-nurturers. There are clearly historical and perhaps even biological explanations for why sex category—whether an individual has a penis or a uterus and accompanying secondary sex characteristics—has been elaborated into cultural manifestations of gender and eventually into a gender structure. I leave that discussion to historians. I am more interested in the future. At this point in history I question the need, indeed the usefulness, of continuing to elaborate on sex category at all. If we are to allow individuals full room to maneuver, to build on their strengths, to create themselves, why shackle any of us with cognitive images that restrict us to gendered notions? Why differentiate at all in the way we socialize girls and boys? Why should sex category matter in determining life chances and social roles, in the family or outside of it?

My answer is that gender should be irrelevant to all aspects of our lives. I am not denying biology. Women give birth and lactate. But in the interests of equity we might create social norms that take for granted that fathers devote the first nine months after birth to their babies insofar as mothers have devoted much time and energy in the nine months preceding the birth. If as a society we begin with the assumption that every paid employee also has, at some point in the life cycle, elderly parents, children, and perhaps ailing partners to care for, we must redesign the demands of employment. Our economic structure currently is built on the invisible, nurturing work of women. If the gender structure is simply deleted from the screen, the expectations that we make of paid workers and the organization of workplaces and schools will need dramatic changes. If we do not presume that women inside the family are responsible for the caregiving and nurturing that we all need, we just might have to integrate the expectation of caring relationships into all aspects of our lives, even in our workplaces (Hays 1996).

But the abolition of our gender structure is considerably more challenging to the status quo than the mere blurring of social roles in our families, and even more challenging than the reorganization of our economy that it would require. Perhaps the most challenging implications of abolishing our gender structure would be to our psyches. We all have much at stake in our gendered identities, beyond our social roles. We not only fill gendered roles, we also do gender in the way we walk and talk and dress and eat and play. Gender, as we do it, is not only about subordination, inequality, and stratification but also about who we are and how we experience our selves and our relationships.

In order to rout out the inequality that is a consequence of gender structure we must challenge what it means to be men and women in the twenty-first century. This may ultimately be liberating for ourselves, our children, and future generations. But the immediate gender vertigo will make us more than dizzy; it may even be disorienting. For our clothes, hairstyles, and jewelry are among the few realms in society in which we are free to play, to fantasize, to be creative. Today there are limits to social acceptability in this creativity; ask any man whose inner self dictates that he wear a skirt to the office, or any woman who chooses to shave her head. But there are relatively few men who prefer skirts and women who prefer a bald head. Most of us enjoy playing with our looks, makeup, and clothes in socially acceptable ways. This is gendered play. For although both men and women may enjoy finding the right earrings, women usually wear at least two of them at a time and in both ears; men usually wear none or decorate only one ear. Presentation of self is one of the areas in which each of us has some autonomy and control, and is allowed the pleasure to play even in adulthood—as long as we stay within gendered parameters.

My guess is that at least some of the deeply felt reaction to changing gendered roles in families or in the workplace springs from the fear of going too far, of denying one of the few means of easily accessible, socially acceptable, nonfattening, healthy pleasures available to us: doing gender in ways we enjoy. Consider that this pleasure in doing gender is intertwined with heterosexual sexuality and even the most dedicated heterosexual feminist perceives a threat to happiness if gender itself is eliminated. Only a very foolish feminist theoretician would put these destabilizing aspects of gender at the center of her agenda for social change.

And yet we cannot have inequality unless we have difference, and these gendered means of pleasure are part and parcel of making biological males and females into what appear to be greatly differentiated, gendered men and women. Different enough to be unequal. This is a conundrum from which I have yet to find escape. I have even delayed finishing this book—waiting, thinking, puzzling, and searching for a logically consistent, sociologically accurate feminist way out. There are simply too few ways in our society for people to use and show their creativity; gendered displays of self have become important for these reasons.

Perhaps what we need to do is strike first, and most directly, at the aspects of the gender structure that directly support stratification—family roles that naturalize wives' economic dependency and men's alienation from nurturing work, an economic structure that assumes that paid workers are not responsible for family work at all, and interpersonal sexism that devalues women's abilities. At the same time, we must destabilize the rules that stigmatize those who choose to break gender displays in their presentations of self, to open up room for bald women and skirted men.

We must remember that gendered displays—as natural as they feel—are socially defined. Despite their nearly identical physical form, skirts are for women, kilts are for men. Women cut, shave, starve, and color their bodies in order to do gender. Biological males and females have to learn how to use cultural symbols to do gender. While transsexuals have to learn to do gender displays considered appropriate for the opposite sex, all of us have to learn to do gender displays appropriate for our own sex. None of these displays are "natural"; all gender is drag (Butler 1990).

Bem (1995) suggests that perhaps an immediate strategy toward equality is to turn up the volume on gender categories. We can explode two gender categories into many if we cross-cut gender, sexual identity, and biological sex. What if we create categories based on more complicated identity matrices than simply two genders? Bem suggests that simply by mixing up sex category (male, female), gender (masculine, feminine, androgynous), and desire (heterosexual, homosexual, bisexual), we will have cracked the logic of dichotomizing people by gender, as eighteen categories would exist—just for starters: masculine lesbians, feminine lesbians, androgynous lesbians, masculine straight men, feminine straight men, androgynous straight men, masculine gay men, feminine gay men, androgynous gay men, masculine straight women, feminine straight women, androgynous straight women, feminine bisexual women, masculine bisexual women, androgynous bisexual women, feminine bisexual men, masculine bisexual men, androgynous bisexual men. My view of gender as infinitely more plastic and complex than a three-category variable makes Bem's proposition overwhelming. How would the math work (gender × sex × sexual identity) when we realize that there are dozens of femininities and masculinities in our culture? For how gender gets done varies dramatically by class, ethnicity, race, region, and age. Still, the notion of exploding categories and allowing much more creativity in self-presentation feels more like liberation than does the deemphasizing of gender that we now pleasure ourselves by doing.

We must also open up to less repressive ways of living, allowing both children and their parents to find other, easily accessible means to use their creativity, their sense of color, coordination, and panache. We must not forget that pleasure matters. For after all, don't we care about inequality because we want to equalize our opportunities for pleasure?

But if we are ever going to move toward a post-gendered family in a post-gendered society—a world where men and women are true equals—how one plays with makeup or clothing or hairstyle should have little to do with whether one has a penis or a uterus or has the capacity to birth a child. For if social roles were not built around sexual category, why would we need to elaborate culturally on the difference between sexual attributes rather than recognize the amazing biological similarities in other dimensions (e.g., two hands, two legs, two eyes, equivalent brains)? Elaborated difference is used to justify inequality (Lorber 1994).

For now, though, I suggest that although we must attack the very existence of a gender structure, we must do so in a way that honors the reality of our own and others' use of gendered play for pleasure. And as we continue in this struggle we must widen our vision to think about pleasure and play and about discovering means to allow more of it in new ways, with new games and new pleasures for a post-gendered society. No one will nor should give up strategies for joy without having some idea of a better way.

If gender were primarily inside us as personalities, or primarily based in interactional stereotypes, or primarily a structure of economic inequality, we could choose one level to attack and hope for dramatic changes. The past twenty years have seen dramatic changes with just such single-minded strategies. We have had some success with assertiveness training, with changing stereotypes, and with fighting for economic equality. For most women today, life has been dramatically different from that of their mothers. And our daughters will inherit not only a different world but an entirely different set of expectations from their parents and teachers than did girls of my generation. And yet I believe that we have come as far as we can with incremental change. To get to the next stage, to move fully toward justice for women and men, we must dare a moment of gender vertigo. My hope is that when the spinning ends we will be in a post-gendered society that is one step closer to a just world.

References

Acker, Joan. 1992. "Gendered Institutions: From Sex Roles to Gendered Institutions." *Contemporary Sociology* 21(5):565-569.

Agassi, Judith Bubler. 1989. "Theories of Gender Equity: Lessons from the Kibbutz." *Gender and Society* 3:160-186.

Alanen, L. 1988. "Rethinking Childhood." *Acta Sociologica* 31:53-67.

Alwin, Duane F., and Robert M. Hauser. 1975. "The Decomposition of Effects in Path Analysis." *American Sociological Review* 10:37-47.

Ambert, A. 1982. "Differences in Children's Behavior Toward Custodial Mothers and Custodial Fathers." *Journal of Marriage and the Family* 44(1):73-86.

Aptheker, Bettina. 1989. *Tapestries of Life: Women's Work, Women's Consciousness, and the Meaning of Daily Experience.* Amherst: University of Massachusetts Press.

Atkinson, Maxine, Barbara Risman, and Stephen Blackwelder. 1992. "Measuring Wives' Material Dependence." Paper presented at an NCFR Theory Construction and Research Methodology Workshop, Orlando, Florida.

Aulette, Judy Root. 1994. *Changing Families.* Belmont, Calif.: Wadsworth.

Bandura, A. 1962. "Social Learning Through Imitation." In *Nebraska Symposium on Motivation,* vol. 10, 211-274, edited by M. Jones. Lincoln: University of Nebraska Press.

————. 1971. *Psychological Modeling: Conflicting Themes.* Chicago: Aldine-Atherton.

Bandura, Albert, and Richard H. Walters. 1963. *Social Learning and Personality.* New York: Holt, Rinehart and Winston.

Baron, James T., and William T. Bielby. 1985. "Organizational Barriers to Gender Equality: Sex Segregation of Jobs and Opportunities." In *Gender and the Life Course,* edited by Alice S. Rossi. New York: Aldine de Gruyter.

Barrera, Mario. 1979. *Race and Class in the Southwest.* Notre Dame: University of Notre Dame Press.

Bem, Sandra L. 1974. "The Measurement of Psychological Androgyny." *Journal of Clinical and Consulting Psychology* 4:155–162.

———. 1977. "On the Utility of Alternative Procedures for Assessing Psychological Androgyny." *Journal of Consulting and Clinical Psychology* 45:196–205.

———. 1993. *The Lenses of Gender: Transforming the Debate on Sexual Inequality.* New Haven: Yale University Press.

———. 1995. "Dismantling Gender Polarization and Compulsory Heterosexuality: Should We Turn the Volume Up or Down?" *Journal of Sex Research* 32:4.

Berardo, Donna, Constance Shehan, and Gerald Leslie. 1987. "A Residue of Tradition: Jobs, Careers, and Spouse's Time in Housework." *Journal of Marriage and the Family* 49:381–390.

Berger, Joseph, Bernard P. Cohen, and Morris Zelditch, Jr. 1972. "Status Characteristics and Social Interaction." *American Sociological Review* 37:241–255.

Berger, Peter L., and Hansfried Kellner. 1974. "Marriage and the Construction of Reality." In *The Family: Its Structures and Functions,* edited by Rose Laub Coser. New York: St. Martin's.

Berk, Sarah Fenstermaker. 1985. *The Gender Factory.* New York: Plenum.

Bernard, Jesse. 1981. "The Good Provider Role." *American Psychologist* 36:1–12.

Bielby, Denise D., and William T. Bielby. 1984. "Work Commitment and Sex-Role Attitudes." *American Sociological Review* 49:234–247.

Blackwelder, Stephen P. 1993. "Duality of Structure in the Reproduction of Race, Class, and Gender Inequality." Paper presented at the Society for the Study of Social Problems Meetings, Miami.

Blaisure, Karen R., and Katherine R. Allen. 1995. "Feminists and the Ideology and Practice of Marriage." *Journal of Marriage and the Family* 57(1):5–?.

Blau, Peter M. 1977. *Inequality and Heterogeneity.* New York: Free Press.

Blumberg, Rae Lesser. 1978. *Stratification: Socioeconomic and Sexual Inequality.* Dubuque, Iowa: W. C. Brown.

———. 1986. "Kibbutz Women from the Fields of Revolution to the Lands of Discontent." In *Women in the World, 1975–1985: The Women's Decade,* edited by Lynne B. Iglitzin and Ruth Ross. Santa Barbara, Calif.: ABC-Clio.

Blumstein, Philip. 1991. "The Production of Selves in Personal Relationships." In *The Self-Society: Dynamic Cognition, Emotion, and Action,* edited by Judith A. Howard and Peter J. Callero. New York: Cambridge University Press.

Blumstein, Philip, and Pepper Schwartz. 1983. *American Couples: Money, Work, and Sex.* New York: William Morrow.

Booth, Alan, and James M. Dabbs, Jr. 1992. "Testosterone and Men's Marriages." *Social Forces* 72(2):463–478.

Borman, K. M., and P. O'Reilly. 1987. "Learning Gender Roles in Three Urban U.S. Kindergarten Classrooms." *Child and Youth Services* 8:43–66.

Bornstein, Marc H., and Michael E. Lamb. 1988. *Developmental Psychology: An Advanced Textbook.* Hillsdale, N.J.: Erlbaum.

Bose, Christine. 1987. "Dual Spheres." In *Analyzing Gender,* edited by Beth B. Hess and Myra Marx Ferree. Newbury Park, Calif.: Sage.

Brewer, Rose. 1989. "Black Women and Feminist Sociology: The Emerging Perspectives." *American Sociologist* 20(1)(Spring):57–90.

Brines, Julie. 1994. "Economic Dependency and the Division of Labor." *American Journal of Sociology* 100(3):652–688.

Burt, Ronald S. 1982. *Toward a Structural Theory of Action.* New York: Academic Press.

Butler, J. 1990. *Gender Trouble: Feminism and the Subversion of Identity.* New York: Routledge.

Cain, Glen George. 1966. *Married Women in the Labor Force: An Economic Analysis.* Chicago: University of Chicago Press.

Camarillo, Albert. 1979. *Chicanos in a Changing Society.* Cambridge: Harvard University Press.

Cancian, Francesca M. 1987. *Love in America*. Cambridge, England: Cambridge University Press.

Chafetz, Janet Saltzman. 1984. *Sex and Advantage: A Comparative Macro-Structural Theory of Sex Stratification*. Totowa, N.J.: Rowman and Allanheld.

Chang, Pi Nian, and Amos S. Deinard. 1982. "Single Father Caretakers: Demographic Characteristics and Adjustment Processes." *American Journal of Orthopsychiatry* 53:236–243.

Cherlin, Andrew J. 1992. *Marriage, Divorce, Remarriage*. Cambridge: Harvard University Press.

Chodorow, Nancy. 1978. *The Reproduction of Mothering*. Berkeley: University of California Press.

———. 1989. *Feminism and Psychoanalytic Theory*. New Haven: Yale University Press.

———. 1994. *Femininities, Masculinities, Sexualities: Freud and Beyond*. Lexington: University Press of Kentucky.

———. 1995. "Gender as a Personal and Cultural Construction." *Signs* 20: 516–544.

Coleman, James S. 1990. "The Rational Reconstruction of Society." *American Sociology Review* 58:1–5.

Collins, Patricia Hill. 1990. *Black Feminist Thought: Knowledge, Consciousness, and the Politics of Empowerment*. Boston: Unwin, Hyman.

Collins, Randall, and Scott Coltrane. 1995. *Sociology of Marriage and the Family*. Chicago: Nelson-Hall.

Coltrane, Scott. 1989. "Household Labor and the Routine Production of Gender." *Social Problems* 36:473–490.

———. 1990. "Birth-Timing and the Division of Labor in Dual-Earner Families." *Journal of Family Issues* 1:157–181.

———. 1996. *Family Man: Fatherhood, Housework, and Gender Equity*. Oxford: Oxford University Press.

Connell, Robert W. 1987. *Gender and Power: Society, the Person, and Sexual Politics*. Stanford, Calif.: Stanford University Press.

———. 1995. *Masculinities*. Berkeley: University of California Press.

Constantinople, Anne. 1979. "Sex Role Acquisition: In Search of the Elephant." *Sex Roles* 5:121-133.

Corsaro, W. A. 1985. *Friendship and Peer Culture in the Early Years*. Norwood, N.J.: Ablex.

Corrin, Chris, ed. 1993. *Superwoman and the Double Burden: Women's Experiences of Change in Central and Eastern Europe and the Former Soviet Union*. Toronto: Second Story Press.

Coser, Rose Laub. 1975. "The Complexity of Roles as a Seedbed of Individual Autonomy." In *Social Structure*, edited by Lewis A. Coser and Robert K. Merton. New York: Harcourt Brace Jovanovich.

Coverman, Shelley. 1983. "Gender, Domestic Labor Time, and Wage Inequality." *American Sociological Review* 48:623-637.

Dabbs, James. 1992. "Testosterone and Occupational Achievement." *Social Forces* 70(3):813-824.

Deaux, Kay. 1984. "From Individual Differences to Social Categories: Analysis of a Decade's Research on Gender." *American Psychologist* 39:105-116.

Deaux, Kay, and Brenda Major. 1990. "A Social-Psychological Model of Gender." In *Theoretical Perspectives on Sexual Difference*, edited by Deborah Rhode. New Haven: Yale University Press.

Deckard, Barbara Sinclair. 1979. *The Women's Movement: Political, Socioeconomic, and Psychological Issues*. New York: Harper and Row.

Defrain, John, and Rod Eirick. 1981. "Coping as Divorced Parents: A Comparative Study of Fathers and Mothers." *Family Relations* 30:265-273.

Della-Fave, L. Richard. 1986. "Toward an Explication of the Legitimation Process." *Social Forces* 65(2):476-500.

Dinnerstein, Dorothy. 1976. *The Mermaid and the Minotaur: Sexual Arrangements and the Human Malaise*. New York: Harper and Row.

Downey, Douglas B., and Brian Powell. 1993. "Do Children in Single-Parent Households Fare Better Living with Same-Sex Parents?" *Journal of Marriage and the Family* 55:55-71.

Eagly, Alice H. 1995. "The Science and Politics of Comparing Women and Men." *American Psychologist* 50(3):145-150.

Eagly, Alice H., and Valerie J. Steffen. 1984. "Gender Stereotypes Stem from the Distribution of Women and Men into Social Roles." *Journal of Personality and Social Psychology* 46:735-754.

Eagly, Alice H., and Wendy Woods. 1991. "Explaining Sex Differences in Social Behavior: A Meta-Analytic Perspective." *Personality and Social Psychology Bulletin* 17(3): 306-315.

Ehrensaft, Diane. 1987. *Parenting Together: Men and Women Sharing the Care of Their Children.* New York: Free Press.

Eisenberg, N., S. A. Wolchik, R. Hernandez, and J. F. Pasternack. 1985. "Parental Socialization of Young Children's Play: A Short-Term Longitudinal Study." *Child Development* 56:1506-1513.

Elshtain, Jean Bethke. 1982. "Feminism, Family, and Community." *Dissent* (Fall):444-449.

England, Paula, and George Farkas. 1980. *Households, Employment, and Gender.* New York: Aldine de Gruyter.

England, Paula, and Irene Browne. 1992. "Internalization and Constraint in Women's Subordination." *Current Perspectives in Social Theory* 12: 97-123.

Epstein, Cynthia Fuchs. 1988. *Deceptive Distinctions: Sex, Gender, and the Social Order.* New Haven: Yale University Press.

Ewer, Phyllis A., Eileen Crimmins, and Richard Oliver. 1979. "An Analysis of the Relationship Between Husband's Income, Family Size, and Wife's Employment in the Early Stages of Marriage." *Journal of Marriage and the Family* 41: 727-738.

Fagot, B. I., M. D. Leinbach, and C. O'Boyle. 1992. "Gender Labeling, Gender Stereotyping, and Parenting Behaviors." *Development Psychology* 28:225-230.

Ferree, Myra Marx. 1990. "Beyond Separate Spheres: Feminism and Family Research." *Journal of Marriage and the Family* 53(4):866-884.

Ferree, Myra Marx, and Beth Hess. 1987. "Introduction." In *Analyzing*

Gender: A Handbook of Social Science Research, edited by Beth Hess and Myra Marx Ferree. Newbury Park, Calif.: Sage.

Ferri, E. 1973. "Characteristics of Motherless Families." *British Journal of Social Work* 3(1):91–100.

Fine, Gary Alan, and Sherryl Kleinman. 1979. "Rethinking Subculture: An Interactionist Analysis." *American Journal of Sociology* 85:1–20.

Friedan, Betty. 1963. *The Feminine Mystique.* New York: Dell.

———. 1981. *The Second Stage.* New York: Summit.

Freud, Sigmund. 1933. "Femininity, in New Introductory Lectures on Psycho-Analysis." 22:112–135 in *Standard Edition of the Complete Psychological Works of Sigmund Freud,* 22:112–135, edited by James Strachey.

Funk, Nanette, and Magda Mueller, eds. 1993. *Gender Politics and Post Communism: Reflections from East Europe and the Former Soviet Union.* New York: Routledge.

Gasser, R. D., and C. H. Taylor. 1976. "Role Adjustment of Single Fathers with Dependent Children." *Family Coordinator* 25(4):397–402.

Geis, Florence L., Virginia Brown, Joyce Jennings, and Denise Corrado-Taylor. 1984. "Sex vs. Status in Sex-Associated Stereotypes." *Sex Roles* 11:771–785.

Gekas, Victor. 1979. "The Influence of Social Class on Socialization." In *Contemporary Theories About the Family,* vol. 1, 365–403, edited by Wesley R. Burr, Reuben Hill, F. Ivan Nye, and Iva L. Reiss. New York: Free Press.

George, V., and P. Wilding. 1972. *Motherless Families.* London: Routledge and Kegan Paul.

Gerhardt, Uta. 1973. "Interpretive Processes in Role Conflict Situations." *Sociology* 7:235–240.

Gerson, Kathleen. 1985. *Hard Choices.* Berkeley: University of California Press.

———. 1990. "Work, Family, and Social Policy." Paper presented at the American Sociological Association Meetings, Washington, D.C.

————. 1993. *No Man's Land.* New York: Basic Books.

Giddens, Anthony. 1979. *Central Problems in Social Theory.* Berkeley: University of California Press.

————. 1984. *The Constitution of Society: Outline of the Theory of Structuration.* Berkeley: University of California Press.

Gilligan, Carol. 1982. *In a Different Voice: Psychological Theory and Women's Development.* Cambridge: Harvard University Press.

Glenn, Evelyn Nakano. 1991. "Racial Ethnic Women's Labor." In *Gender, Family, and Economy,* edited by Rae Lesser Blumberg. Newbury Park, Calif.: Sage.

Goode, William J. 1960. "A Theory of Role Strain." *American Sociological Review* 24:38–47.

————. 1964. *The Family.* Englewood Cliffs, N.J.: Prentice-Hall.

Granovetter, Mark. 1985. "Economic Action, Social Structure, and Embeddedness." *American Journal of Sociology* 91:481–510.

Greenberg, J. B. 1979. "Single-Parenting and Intimacy: A Comparison of Mothers and Fathers." *Alternative Lifestyles* 2(3):308–330.

Greenstein, Theodore. 1986. "Human Capital, Marital and Birth Timing, and the Postnatal Labor Force Participation of Married Women." *Journal of Marriage and the Family* 48:565–571.

Grief, Geoffrey. 1985. *Single Fathers.* Lexington, Mass.: Lexington Books.

Haas, Linda. 1980. "Determinants of Role-Sharing Behavior: A Study of Egalitarian Couples." *Sex Roles* 8(7).

————. 1982. "Role-Sharing Couples: A Study of Egalitarian Marriages." *Family Relations* 29:289–296.

————. 1992. *Equal Parenthood and Social Policy.* Albany: State University of New York Press.

Hall, Leslie D., Alexis J. Walker, and Alan C. Acock. 1995. "Gender and Family Work in One-Parent Households." *Journal of Marriage and the Family* 57:685–692.

Handel, Warren. 1979. "Normative Expectations and the Emergence of Meaning as Solutions to Problems: Convergence of Structural and Interactionist Views." *American Journal of Sociology* 84(4):855–881.

Hanson, Shirley M. H. 1981. "Single Custodial Fathers and the Parent-Child Relationship." *Nursing Research* 30:202-204.

———. 1986. "Healthy Single-Parent Families." *Family Relations* 35: 125-132.

Hartmann, Heidi I. 1981. "The Family as the Locus of Gender, Class, and Political Struggle: The Example of Housework." *Signs* 6:366-394.

Hawkins, J. 1985. "Computers and Girls: Rethinking the Issues." *Sex Roles* 13:165-180.

Hayghe, Howard, and Suzanne M. Bianchi. 1994. "Married Mothers' Work Patterns: The Job-Family Compromise." *Monthly Labor Review* 117(6):24-30.

Hays, Sharon. 1996. *The Cultural Contradictions of Motherhood.* New Haven: Yale University Press.

Hazleton, Lesley. 1977. *Israeli Women: The Reality Behind the Myths.* New York, N.Y.: Simon and Schuster.

Heiss, Jerold. 1981. "Social Rules." In *Social Psychology: Sociological Perspectives,* edited by Morris Rosenberg and Ralph H. Turner. New York: Basic Books.

Henley, Nancy M. 1977. *Body Politics: Power, Sex, and Nonverbal Communication.* Englewood Cliffs, N.J.: Prentice-Hall.

Hertz, Rosanna. 1986. *More Equal Than Others: Women and Men in Dual-Career Marriages.* Berkeley: University of California Press.

Hewitt, John P. 1979. *Self and Society: A Symbolic Interactionist Social Psychology.* Boston: Allyn and Bacon.

Hipgrave, T. 1982. "Lone Fatherhood: A Problematic Status." In *The Father Figure,* 171-183, edited by L. McKee and M. O'Brien. London: Tavistock.

Hochschild, Arlie Russell. 1989. *The Second Shift: Working Parents and the Revolution at Home.* New York: Viking.

hooks, bell. 1984. *Feminist Theory: From Margin to Center.* Boston: South End Press.

Howard, Judith, Barbara Risman, Mary Romero, and Joey Sprague. 1996.

The Gender Lens Series. Newbury Park, Calif.: Sage Publications and Pine Forge Press.

Howard, Ann, and D. W. Bray. 1988. *Managerial Lives in Transition: Advancing Age and Changing Times.* New York: Guilford Press.

Hughes, Everett C. 1945. "Dilemmas and Contradictions of Status." *American Journal of Sociology* 50:353–359.

Hunt, Janet, and Larry L. Hunt. 1977. "The Dilemmas and Contradictions of Status: The Case of the Dual-Career Family." *Social Problems* 24(4):407–416.

Hutson, A. H. 1983. "Sex-Typing." In *Handbook of Child Psychology,* vol. 4, edited by E. M. Hetherington. New York: Wiley.

Inglehart, Ronald. 1977. *The Silent Revolution: Changing Values and Political Styles among Western Publics.* Princeton, N.J.: Princeton University Press.

———. 1981. "Post-Materialism in an Environment of Insecurity." *American Political Science Review* 75:880–900.

Inkeles, A. 1968. "Society, Social Structure, and Child Socialization." In *Socialization and Society,* edited by J. Clausen. Boston: Little, Brown.

Jacobs, Jerry A. 1989. *Revolving Doors in Sex Segregation and Women's Careers.* Stanford, Calif.: Stanford University Press.

Jaggar, Alison M., and Paula Rothenberg Struhl. 1978. *Feminist Frameworks.* New York: McGraw-Hill.

Jones, Jacqueline. 1985. *Labor of Love, Labor of Sorrow.* New York: Basic Books.

Kanter, Rosabeth. 1977. *Men and Women of the Corporation.* New York: Harper and Row.

Katz, A. J. 1979. "Lone Fathers: Perspectives and Implications for Family Policy." *Family Coordinator* 28(4):521–528.

Keller, Evelyn Fox. 1985. *Reflections on Gender and Science.* New Haven: Yale University Press.

Kimball, Gayle. 1983. *50–50 Marriage.* Boston: Beacon Press.

King, Deborah K. 1988. "Multiple Jeopardy, Multiple Consciousness: The Context of a Black Feminist Ideology." *Signs* 14:42–72.

Kohlberg, Lawrence. 1966. "A Cognitive-Developmental Analysis of Children's Sex-Role Concepts and Attitudes." In *The Development of Sex Differences*, 82-172, edited by Eleanor Maccoby. Stanford, Calif.: Stanford University Press.

Kohn, Melvin. 1969. *Class and Conformity.* Homewood, Ill.: Dorsey.

————. 1979. "The Effects of Social Class on Parental Values and Practices." In *The American Family: Dying or Developing?* 45-68, edited by David Reiss and Howard Hoffman. New York: Plenum.

Kollock, Peter, Phillip Blumstein, and Pepper Schwartz. 1985. "Sex and Power in Interaction: Conversational Privileges and Duties." *American Sociological Review* 50:34-46.

Komarovsky, Mirra. 1967. *Blue-Collar Marriage.* New York: Random House.

Kreps, G. A., and S. L. Bosworth with J. A. Mooney, S. T. Russell, and K. A. Myers. 1994. *Organizing, Role Enactment, and Disaster: A Structural Theory.* Newark: University of Delware Press.

Kuhn, Manford H. 1960. "Self Attitudes by Age, Sex and Professional Training." *Sociological Quarterly* 1:39-55.

Kuh, Manford H., and Thomas S. McPartland. 1954. "An Empirical Investigation of Self Attitudes." *American Sociological Review* 19:58-76.

Lasch, Christopher. 1977. *Haven in a Heartless World.* New York: Basic Books.

Laws, Judith Long. 1979 *The Second X: Sex Role and Social Role.* New York: Elsevier Science.

Lee, Richard B. 1992. "Art, Science, or Politics." *American Anthropologist* 94:31-51.

Lee, Richard B. *The !Kung San: Men, Women, and Work in a Foraging Society.* Cambridge: Cambridge University Press.

Lennon, Mary C., and Sarah Rosenfeld. 1994. "Relative Fairness and the Division of Housework: The Importance of Options." *American Journal of Sociology* 100(2):506-531.

Lenski, Gerhardt, and Jean Lenski. 1974. *Human Societies.* New York: McGraw-Hill.

Lerner, Gerda. 1986. *The Creation of Patriarchy*. New York: Oxford University Press.

Lesthaeghe, Ron. 1980. "On the Social Control of Human Reproduction." *Population and Development Review* 4:427-548.

Lever, Janet. 1976. "Sex Differences in the Games Children Play." *Social Problems* 23:479-489.

————. 1978. "Sex Differences in the Complexity of Children's Play and Games." *American Sociological Review* 43:471-483.

Lewis, Michael. 1972. "There's No Unisex in the Nursery." *Psychology Today* 5:54-57.

Lewis, Michael, and Marsha Weinraub. 1979. "Origins of Early Sex Role Development." *Sex Roles* 5:135-155.

Lorber, Judith. 1981. "On the Reproduction of Mothering: A Methodological Debate." *Signs* 6:482-486.

————. 1984. *Women Physicians: Career, Status, and Power*. London: Tavistock.

————. 1986. "Dismantling Noah's Ark." *Sex Roles* 14:567-580.

————. 1994. *Paradoxes of Gender*. New Haven: Yale University Press.

Luepnitz, Deborah Anna. 1986. "A Comparison of Maternal, Parental, and Joint Custody: Understanding the Varieties of Post-Divorce Family Life." *Journal of Divorce* 9(3):1-12.

Lunneborg, Patricia. 1990. *Women Changing Work*. New York: Bergin and Garvey.

Luttrell, W. 1993. "The Teachers, They All Had Their Pets: Concepts of Gender, Knowledge, and Power." *Signs* 18:505-546.

Maccoby, E. E. 1992. "The Role of Parents in the Socialization of Children: An Historical Overview." *Developmental Psychology* 28:1006-1017.

Maccoby, Eleanor E., and Carolyn N. Jacklin. 1974. *The Psychology of Sex Differences*. Stanford, Calif.: Stanford University Press.

McHugh, Peter. 1968. *Defining the Situation*. Indianapolis: Bobbs-Merrill.

MacKinnon, Catherine A. 1982. "Feminism, Marxism, Method, and the State: An Agenda for Theory." *Signs* 7:514–544.

McLaughlin, Steven D. 1982. "Differential Patterns of Female Labor Force Participation Surrounding the First Birth." *Journal of Marriage and the Family.* New York: Free Press.

McMahon, Martha. 1995. *Engendering Motherhood.* New York: Guilford.

Margolis, Maxine L. 1984. *Mothers and Such: Views of American Women and Why They Changed.* Berkeley: University of California Press.

Marks, Carole. 1985. "Black Workers and the Great Migration North." *Phylon* 46(2):148–161.

Martin, C. L. 1993. "New Directions for Investigating Children's Gender Knowledge." *Developmental Review* 13:184–204.

Mayhew, Bruce H. 1980. "Structuralism versus Individuals: Part I, Shadow Boxing in the Dark." *Social Forces* 59:335–375.

Meeker, B. F., and P. A. Weitzel-O'Neill. 1977. "Sex Roles and Interpersonal Behavior in Task-Oriented Groups." *American Sociological Review* 42:91–105.

Mendes, H. A. 1979. "Single-Parent Families—A Typology of Lifestyles." *Social Work* 24(3):193–200.

Merton, Robert K. 1948. "The Self-Fulfilling Prophesy." *Antioch Review* 8:193–210.

———. 1975. "Structural Analysis in Sociology." In *Approaches to the Study of Social Structure,* 21–51, edited by Peter M. Blau. New York: Free Press.

Mies, Maria. 1986. *Patriarchy and Accumulation on a World Scale: Women in the International Division of Labour.* Atlantic Highlands, N.J.: Zed Books.

Mintz, Stephen, and Susan Kellogg. 1988. *Domestic Revolutions: A Social History of American Family Life.* New York: Free Press.

Mischel, Walter. 1966. "A Social Learning View of Sex Differences in Behavior." In *The Development of Sex Differences,* 56–81, edited by Eleanor Maccoby. Stanford, Calif.: Stanford University Press.

Modell, John, and Tamara Hareven. 1978. "Urbanization and the Malleable Household." In *The American Family in Social Historical Perspective,* edited by Michael Gordon. New York: St. Martin's.

Murch, M. 1973. "Motherless Families Project: Bristol Council of Social Service Report on First Year's Work." *British Journal of Social Work* 3(3):365-376.

Norton, Arthur J., and Paul C. Glick. 1986. "One-Parent Families: A Social and Economic Profile." *Family Relations* 35:9-17.

O'Brien, Mary. 1982. "Becoming a Lone Father: Differential Patterns and Experiences." In *The Father Figure,* 184-207, edited by L. McKee and M. O'Brien. London: Tavistock.

———. 1983. *The Politics of Reproduction.* Boston: Routledge and Kegan Paul.

Okin, Susan Moller. 1989. *Justice, Gender, and the Family.* New York: Basic Books.

Orlofsky, Jacob L., Alice L. Aslin, and Shelia D. Ginsburg. 1977. "Differential Effectiveness of Two Classification Procedures on the Bem Sex Role Inventory." *Journal of Assessment* 41:414-15.

Orthner, Dennis K., Terry Brown, and Dennis Ferguson. 1976. "Single-Parent Fatherhood: An Emerging Family Lifestyle." *Family Coordinator* 25:429-437.

Otto, Luther B., Vaughn R. A. Call, and Kenneth Spenner. 1981. *Design for a Study of Entry into Careers.* Lexington, Mass.: Lexington Books.

Parsons, Talcott. 1954. *Family Socialization and Interaction Process.* Glencoe, Ill.: Free Press.

Parsons, T., and R. Bales. 1955. *Family Socialization and Interaction Process.* Glencoe, Ill.: Free Press.

Peterson, G. W., and B. C. Rollins. 1987. "Parent-Child Socialization." In *Handbook of Marriage and the Family,* edited by M. Sussman and S. Steinmetz. New York: Plenum.

Pett, Marjorie A., and Beth Vaughan-Cole. 1986. "The Impact of Income Issues and Social Status on Post-Divorce Adjustment of Custodial Parents." *Family Relations* 35:1.

Piaget, J. 1932. *The Moral Judgement of the Child.* London: Kegan Paul.

Pleck, Joseph, and Jack Sawyer, eds. 1974. *Men and Masculinity.* Englewood Cliffs, N.J.: Prentice-Hall.

Poloma, Margaret M. 1972. "Role Conflict and the Married Professional Woman." In *Toward a Sociology of Women,* edited by Constantina Safilios-Rothschild. Lexington, Mass.: Xerox College Publishing.

Poloma, Margaret M., and T. Neal Garland. 1971. "The Married Professional Woman: A Study in the Tolerance of Domestication." *Journal of Marriage and the Family* 33(3):531–540.

Posadskaya, Anastasia. 1991. "Changes in Gender Discourses and Policies." Paper presented at the U.N. University/WIDER Research Conference on "Gender and Restructuring; Perestroika, the 1989 Revolution and Women," Helsinki.

Pruett, Kyle D. 1987. *The Nurturing Father.* New York: Warner Books.

Rapoport, Rhona, and Robert Rapoport. 1972. "Dual-Career Pattern: A Variant Pattern and Social Change." In *Toward a Sociology of Women,* edited by Constantina Safilios-Rothschild. Lexington, Mass.: Xerox College Publishing.

———. 1980. "The Generations of Dual-Career Family Research." In *Dual-Career Couples,* edited by Fran Pepitone-Rockwell. Beverly Hills, Calif.: Sage.

Renzetti, C. M., and D. J. Curran. 1992. *Women and Men in Society.* Boston: Allyn and Bacon.

Reskin, Barbara. 1988. "Bringing the Men Back In: Sex Differentiation and the Devaluation of Women's Work." *Gender and Society* 2:58–81.

———. 1989. Review of *Deceptive Distinctions: Sex, Gender, and the Social Order,* by Cynthia Fuchs Epstein. *Contemporary Sociology* 18: 690–691.

———. 1992. "Gender Jobs and the Language of Choice." Paper presented at the Conference on Gender as a Social Concept. Somerset, Pa.

Reskin, Barbara, and Irene Padavic. 1994. *Women and Men at Work.* Thousand Oaks, Calif.: Pine Forge Press.

178 References

Richardson, L. W. 1981. *The Dynamics of Sex and Gender.* 2nd ed. Boston: Houghton-Mifflin.

Ridgeway, Cecilia. 1982. "Status in Groups: The Importance of Motivation." *American Sociological Review* 47:76–88.

———. 1997. "Interaction and the Conservation of Gender Inequality: Considering Employment." *American Sociological Review* 62:218–235.

Risman, Barbara. 1988. "Just the Two of Us: Parent-Child Relationships in Single Parent Homes." *Journal of Marriage and the Family* 50:1049–1062.

———. 1987. "Intimate Relationships from a Microstructural Perspective: Mothering Men." *Gender and Society* 1:6–32.

———. 1986. "Can Men 'Mother'?: Life as a Single Father." *Family Relations* 35:95–102.

Risman, Barbara, Maxine Atkinson, and Stephen Blackwelder. 1994. "Are Hard Choices Really Choices?" Paper presented at the American Sociological Association Meetings, Los Angeles.

———. 1998. "Understanding the Juggling Act: Gender-Role Socialization versus Social Structural Constraints." *Sociological Forum* 14.

Risman, Barbara, and Danette Johnson-Sumerford. 1997. "Doing It Fairly: A Study of Feminist Marriages." *Journal of Marriage and the Family* 60(1).

Risman, Barbara, and Kristen Myers. 1997. "As the Twig Is Bent: Children Reared in Feminist Households." *Qualitative Sociology* 20:2.

Risman, Barbara, and Pepper Schwartz. 1989. *Gender in Intimate Relationships.* Belmont, Calif.: Wadsworth.

Roby, Pamela. 1992. "Women and the ASA: Degendering Organizational Structures and Processes." *American Sociologist* 23:18–32.

Rosen, R. 1979. "Children of Divorce." *Canadian Journal of Family Law* 2:403–415.

Rosenberg, Morris. 1981. "The Self-Concept." In *Social Psychology: Sociological Perspectives,* 593–634, edited by Morris Rosenberg and Ralph H. Turner. New York: Basic Books.

Rosenfield, Rachel A. 1979. "Women's Occupational Careers: Individual and Structural Explanations." *Sociology of Work and Occupations* 6: 283–311.

Rosenthal, K., and H. F. Keshet. 1981. *Fathers Without Partners.* Totowa, N.J.: Rowan and Littlefield.

Rosenthal, Robert, and Lenore Jacobson. 1968. *Pygmalion in the Class-room: Teacher Expectations and Pupil's Intellectual Development.* New York: Holt, Rinehart and Winston.

Rossi, Alice. 1977. "A Biosocial Perspective on Parenting." *Daedalus* 106(2):1–32.

———. 1984. "Gender and Parenthood." *American Sociological Review* 49:1–19.

Rubin, Gayle. 1975. "The Traffic in Women: Notes on the Political Economy of Sex." In *Toward an Anthropology of Women,* 157–210, edited by Rayna R. Reiter. New York: Monthly Review Press.

Rubin, Lillian B. 1976. *Worlds of Pain: Life in the Working-Class Family.* New York: Basic Books.

———. 1982. *Intimate Strangers.* New York: Harper and Row.

———. 1990. *Erotic Wars: What Happened to the Sexual Revolution?* New York: Farrar, Straus and Giroux.

Ruble, Diane N. 1984. "Sex-Role Development." In *Developmental Psychology: An Advanced Textbook,* 325–371, edited by N. Marc Bornstein and Michael E. Lamb. Hillsdale, N.J.: Erlbaum.

Ruddick, Sara. 1989. *Maternal Thinking.* Boston: Beacon Press.

———. 1992. "Thinking About Fathers." In *Rethinking the Family: Some Feminist Questions,* edited by Barrie Thorne. Boston: Northeastern University Press.

Russell, Graeme. 1983. *The Changing Role of Fathers.* St. Lucia, Australia: University of Queensland Press.

Rytina, Steve, Peter Blau, Jenny Blum, and Joseph Schwartz. 1988. "Inequality and Intermarriage: Paradox of Motive and Constraint." *Social Forces* 66:645–675.

Sacks, Karen. 1984. "Generations of Working-Class Families." In *My Troubles Are Going to Have Trouble with Me: Everyday Trials and Tri-*

umphs of Women Workers, edited by Karen B. Sacks and Dorothy Remy. New Brunswick, N.J.: Rutgers University Press.

Santrock, J., and R. A. Warshak. 1979. "Father Custody and Social Development in Boys and Girls." *Journal of Social Issues* 35(4):112-125.

Santrock, J., R. Warshak, and G. Elliot. 1982. "Social Development and Parent-Child Interaction in Father Custody and Stepmother Families." In *Nontraditional Families: Parenting and Child Development,* edited by Michael E. Lamb. Hillsdale, N.J.: Erlbaum.

Schnayer, Reuben, and R. Robert Orr. 1989. "A Comparison of Children Living in Single-Mother and Single-Father Families." *Journal of Divorce* 12:171-184.

Schwalbe, Michael L. 1987. "Mead Among the Cognitivists: Role as Performance Imaginary." *Journal for the Theory of Social Behavior* 17:113-133.

Schwartz, Pepper. 1994. *Peer Marriage: How Love Between Equals Really Works.* New York: Free Press.

Segal, L. 1990. *Slow Motion: Changing Masculinities, Changing Men.* New Brunswick, N.J.: Rutgers University Press.

Shorter, Edward. 1975. *The Making of the Modern Family.* New York: Basic Books.

Signorelli, N. 1990. "Children, Television, and Gender Roles." *Journal of Adolescent Health Care* 11:50-58.

Skolnick, Arlene. 1991. *Embattled Paradise.* New York: Basic Books.

Smelser, Neil J. 1988. "Social Structure." In *Handbook of Sociology,* edited by Neil J. Smelser. Beverly Hills, Calif.: Sage.

Smith, Dorothy E. 1987. *The Everyday World as Problematic: A Feminist Sociology.* Boston: Northeastern University Press.

Smith, R., and C. Smith. 1981. "Child Rearing and Single-Parent Fathers." *Family Relations* 30:411-417.

Smith-Lovin, Lynn, and Ann R. Tickamyer. 1978. "Nonrecursive Models of Labor Force Participation, Fertility Behavior, and Sex Role Attitudes." *American Sociological Review* 43:541-557.

South, Scott J., and Glenna Spitz. 1994. "Housework in Marital and Non-marital Households." *American Sociological Review* 59:327–347.

Sprague, Joey. 1988. "The Other Side of the Banner: Toward a Feminization of Politics." In *Seeing Female: Social Roles and Personal Lives,* 159–171, edited by Sharon S. Brehm. New York: Greenwood Press.

———. 1991. "Gender, Class, and Political Thinking." *Research in Political Sociology* 5: 111–139.

Stacey, Judith. 1983. "The New Conservative Feminism." *Feminist Studies* 9:559–583.

———. 1990. *Brave New Families.* New York: Basic Books.

Stern M., and K. H. Karraker. 1989. "Sex Stereotyping of Infants: A Review of Gender Labeling Studies." *Sex Roles* 20:501–522.

Stokes, Randall, and John Hewitt. 1976. "Aligning Actions." *American Sociological Review* 41:838–849.

Strahan, Robert F. 1975. "Remarks on Bem's Measurement of Psychological Androgyny." *Journal of Consulting and Clinical Psychology* 43:568–571.

Strauss, Anselm. 1969. *Mirrors and Masks: Transformations of Identity.* New York: Macmillan.

Stryker, Sheldon. 1980. *Symbolic Interactionism: A Social Structural View.* Menlo Park, Calif.: Benjamin-Cummings.

———. 1981. "Symbolic Interactionism: Themes and Variations." In *Sociological Perspectives,* edited by Morris Rosenberg and Ralph H. Turner. New York: Basic Books.

Sweet, James A. 1973. *Women in the Labor Force.* New York: Seminar Press.

Sweet, James, Larry Bumpass, and Vaughn Call. 1988. "The Design and Content of the National Survey of Families and Households." Madison, Wis.: Center for Demography and Ecology.

Symons, Donald. 1979. *The Evolution of Human Sexuality.* New York: Oxford University Press.

Tannen, Deborah. 1990. *You Just Don't Understand.* New York: Ballantine.

Tavris, Carol, and Carole Offir. 1977. *The Longest War: Sex Differences in Perspectives*. New York: Harcourt Brace Jovanovich.

Thompson, Elizabeth, Sara S. McLanahan, and Roberta Braun Curtin. 1992. "Family Structure, Gender, and Parental Socialization." *Journal of Marriage and the Family* 54(2):368–378.

Thompson, Linda. 1991. "Family Work: Women's Sense of Fairness." *Journal of Family Issues* 12:181–196.

Thompson, Martha E. 1981. "Sex Differences: Differential Access to Power or Sex-Role Socialization?" *Sex Roles* 7:413–424.

Thorne, Barrie. 1993. *Gender Play*. New Brunswick, N.J.: Rutgers University Press.

U.S. Department of Commerce, Bureau of Census. 1980. "Household and Family Characteristics: March 1979." *Current Population Reports*. Washington, D.C.: U.S. Government Printing Office.

U.S. Department of Commerce, Bureau of the Census. 1992. "Special Studies." *Current Population Reports*, p. 23. Washington, D.C.: U.S. Government Printing Office.

U.S. Department of Commerce, Bureau of the Census, 1995. *Statistical Abstracts of the United States: 1995* (115th ed.), p. 491. Washington, D.C.: U.S. Government Printing Office.

Udry, J. Richard, and Luther Talbert. 1988. "Sex Hormone Effects on Personality at Puberty." *Journal of Personality and Social Psychology* 54:291–295.

Van den Berghe, Pierre L. 1979. *Human Family Systems: An Evolutionary View*. New York: Elsevier.

Vander Zanden, J. W. 1985. *Human Development*. New York: Knopf.

Wagner, David G., Rebecca S. Ford., and Thomas W. Ford. 1986. "Can Gender Inequalities Be Reduced?" *American Sociological Review* 51: 47–60.

Waite, Linda, and Ross M. Stolzenberg. 1976. "Intended Childbearing and Labor Force Participation of Young Women." *American Sociological Review* 41:235–252.

Warshak, Richard A. 1986. "Father-Custody and Child Development: A

Review and Analysis of Psychological Research." *Behavioral Science and the Law* 4:185-202.

Warshak, Richard, and John W. Santrock. 1983. "Children of Divorce: Impact of Custody Disposition on Social Development." In *Life Span Developmental Psychology: Nonnormative Life Events,* edited by Edward J. Callahan and Kathleen A. McClusky. New York: Academic Press.

Weitzman, Lenore Jacqueline. 1979. *Sex Role Socialization: A Focus on Women.* Palo Alto, Calif.: Mayfield.

Welter, Barbara. 1973. "The Cult of True Womanhood: 1820-1860." In *The American Family in Social-Historical Perspective,* edited by Michael Gordon. New York: St. Martin's.

West, Candace, and Don H. Zimmerman. 1987. "Doing Gender." *Gender and Society* 1(2):125-151.

West, Candace, and Sarah Fenstermaker. 1995. "Doing Difference." *Gender and Society* 9:8-37.

Wilder, G., D. Mackie, and J. Cooper. 1985. "Gender and Computers: Two Surveys of Gender-Related Attitudes." *Sex Roles* 13:215-228.

Williams, Christine. 1989. *Gender Differences at Work.* Berkeley: University of California Press.

————. 1992. "The Glass Escalator: Hidden Advantages for Men in the 'Female' Professions." *Social Problems* 39:253-267.

————. 1993. "Psychoanalytic Theory and the Sociology of Gender." In *Theory on Gender/Feminism on Theory,* edited by Paula England. New York: Aldine de Gruyter.

Wilson, Edward O. 1975. *Sociobiology: The New Synthesis.* Cambridge: Belknap.

————. 1978. *On Human Nature.* Cambridge: Harvard University Press.

Wrong, Dennis H. 1961. "The Oversocialized Conception of Man in Modern Sociology." *American Sociological Review* 26:183-193.

Yoder, Janice. 1991. "Rethinking Tokenism: Looking Beyond Numbers." *Social Problems* 5:178-192.

Zimmer, Lynn. 1988. "Tokenism and Women in the Workplace: The Limits of Gender-Neutral Theory." *Social Problems* 35:64-77.

Index

Acock, Alan C., 69-70
androcentrism, 2-3
Atkinson, Maxine, 9, 73-74, 75-91

Bem, Sandra L., 2-3, 6, 10, 56, 132, 134, 160
Bem Sex Role Inventory (BSRI), 56-58
Berk, Sarah Fenstermaker, 4, 47, 57. *See also* Fenstermaker
Blackwelder, Stephen, 9, 28, 73-74, 75-91
Blau, Peter M., 26-27
Blumstein, Philip, 93, 96-98
Browne, Irene, 24-25
Burt, Ronald S., 26-27
Butler, J. *See* gender, deconstruction of

Career Development Study, 76
cathexis, 118-20; defined, 105. *See also* Connell
child care, 7, 39-41, 48-50, 56, 72-74, 87, 95-96, 110. *See also* families; children
childrearing. *See* families; children
children: daily activities of, 131-35, 136-42; development of identity in, 129-34, 142-47; ideology of, 135-36, 148-50; in fair families, 134-47; in single-parent homes, 50-54, 57-70, 153-54; socialization of, 128, 130-34, 136-47, 153-54, 157-59. *See also* mothering; fathers, single

children's perceptions of gender. *See* gender
Chodorow, Nancy, 15-16, 24-25, 47, 58
class (middle, working), 9, 11-12, 20-22, 24, 30-31, 49-50, 54-55, 72-76, 82, 85, 87-91, 97, 101-2, 114, 126-29, 154-55. *See also* families, fair, economic status of
cognitive images, 32-33, 35, 41-42, 58, 149-56
Coltrane, Scott, 90, 91, 96, 134, 156
Connell, Robert W., 6, 14, 17, 27-28, 103-5, 118-19, 134, 151
control, 115-18; defined, 105. *See also* Connell
cultural component of gender, 31-35, 74-82, 128
Curtin, Roberta Braun, 68-69

Deaux, Kay, 23
doing gender, 4, 6-7, 10, 22-24, 32-33, 37, 159
Downey, Douglas B., 51-52
dual-career couples, 33, 47, 93-98. *See* marriage; families, fair
dual-earner marriages. *See* marriage; families, fair
dual-nurturer marriages. *See* marriage; families, fair

Eagly, Alice H., 18-19, 30n
economic institutions, 154-57, 160-61

Giddens, Anthony, 27

Hall, Leslie D., 69–70
Handel, Warren, 31
Hanson, Shirley, 51
Hertz, Rosanna, 22, 95
Hewitt, John, 31
Hochschild, Arlie Russell, 33, 48, 57, 109, 119
housework, breakdown by gender, 4, 32, 36–37, 49, 56, 59–65, 69–70, 93–98, 106–14, 116–18. See also labor

individual level theory, 13, 16–17, 28–31, 48, 58, 60–61, 67, 126, 129, 147–49, 151–53, 156; biological, 3, 13–14; essentialist, 2–4, 14; psychoanalytical, 3, 15–16; sex-role socialization, 16–18
institutional level theory, 7, 19–22, 23–24, 28–34, 35, 38–43, 103–5, 118, 126–27, 129, 147–49, 151–53, 155–59; structural, 19–21, 24–31
interactional level theory, 6, 10, 23–24, 28–34, 35, 38–43, 45–49, 58, 60–61, 67, 83–84, 91, 103–5, 126–27, 129, 147–49, 151–53, 155–56. See also doing gender; expectations, based on gender

Jacklin, Carolyn N., 18n
Johnson-Sumerford, Danette, 9, 98–106
juggling paid and family work, 9, 21, 47–48, 55–67, 72–74, 84–87, 93, 154–57. See also labor

Kanter, Rosabeth, 19, 20–22, 24
kibbutzim, gender structure in, 7
Kohlberg, Lawrence, 129–30

labor, 105–15; defined, 105, see also Connell; full-time, 37–40, 54, 72–74 77–82, 83–85, 87–91, 106–14, see also Gerson; household, see housework; paid vs. domestic, see juggling paid and family work; part-time, 40–42, 72–73, 77–82, 83–85, 87–99
labor force participation, 7, 20–22, 84–87, 90–91, 93, 155–56. See also labor
Lennon, Mary C., 41
Lever, Janet, 133–34
Lorber, Judith, 4, 6, 20, 24–25, 156, 161

Maccoby, Eleanor E., 18n
McLanahan, Sara S., 68–69
Major, Brenda, 23
marriage: dual-earner, 47–48, 53, 82, 85–91, 93–98, 106–10, see also families, fair; dual-nurturer, 35–43, 95–96, 106, 110; egalitarian, 35–43, 93–103, 151–62; male dominance in, 11–12, 35–38, 115–16, 126–27, 155, see also marriage, traditional; non-traditional, 111–12, 151–62, see also families, fair; stratification in, 35–43, see also expectations, based on gender; traditional, 45–46, 51–54, 77–82, 85–91, 98, 118–19, 125–27; masculinity, 10, 58, 61–67, 126, 131–33, 134, 137–43, 154, 160–61
maternal thinking, 16. See also Ruddick